"Well-researched, well-argued, and well-balanced, this composite but unified work forms a valuable contribution not only to the discussion of distance education but also to the general issues of the theory and practice of teaching and learning, including pedagogy and andragogy, into which the strengths and weaknesses of distance learning are properly placed. The authors move from biblical foundations for spiritual formation and insights from Paul's epistolary form of 'distance ed' to a plethora of practical applications that extend far beyond technology, with a focus on the best strategies, tools, and environments for successful learning, including intentional faculty development, whatever the specific goals and contexts may be. An excellent resource for veteran and neophyte alike!"

—Andrew H. Bartelt, Gustav and Sophie Butterbach Professor of Exegetical Theology, and vice president for academic affairs (retired), Concordia Seminary

"Grounded firmly in historical perspective, biblical fidelity, and theological conviction, *Teaching the World* is at the vanguard of online theological education. This book fills a desperate need for institutions and educators venturing into digital learning. *Teaching the World* faces online education challenges head-on, unflinchingly. It provides guidance and perspective to those fearing that online education is necessarily impersonal, inadequate, or inferior to traditional learning. *Teaching the World* builds common ground and easy on-ramps for professors struggling to enter the distributive learning fray. These helps, in addition to providing tips for spiritual formation and best practices in online learning, make this book an essential text for professors and administrators alike."

—Freddy Cardoza, executive director, Society of Professors in Christian Education, and director, Christian Education Programs, Talbot School of Theology, Biola University

"The history of innovation is littered with life-altering advances that outpace society's willingness to consider *why* before *what*. Before scrutinizing the second- and third-order effects of a breakthrough as progressive as online education, many well-meaning pragmatists simply assume we *must* employ it just because we *can*. Seldom has such pragmatism been more risky than banking a generation of ministerial training on the promise of new technology without first viewing it through the prism of old theology. *Teaching the World* provides a welcome speed bump to help educators and their customers carefully examine the foundational premises, pros, cons, and best practices of theological education conducted largely online. Since the products of any such program are pastors who will themselves teach the world, the stakes are too high to proceed without first devouring this long-overdue contribution to the education conversation. While my views are my own and do not represent the views of the United States Air Force or the Department of Defense, I strongly recommend this volume."

— Chaplain, Major General Dondi E. Costin

"*Teaching the World* is a deeply refreshing and much needed discussion on the place of online education in theological institutions. The authors prove that such endeavors have a far stronger pedagogical and theological basis than most critics are willing to admit, and that most advocates have put forth. With theological critics of online education, they challenge the purely pragmatic motives that have tended to dominate seminaries and Christian colleges and universities in recent history. But more importantly, they construct a biblical and theological foundation for theological education that gives appropriate place to online education without undermining or neglecting residential models. This is an extremely valuable resource, and I highly recommend it to administrators, faculty, and even critics of online education!"

— James K. Dew Jr., vice president for undergraduate studies and distance learning, associate professor of philosophy and the History of Ideas, Southeastern Baptist Theological Seminary

"Online instruction is a challenge for institutions and faculty as well as students. This book grounds online instruction in a biblical-theological context as a means of fulfilling the mission and mandate of the church. It is theological, theoretical, and practically insightful. It would be difficult to identify another book that provides such an integrated and thorough treatment of the subject, all with a connection to Christian thought and applications. It is indeed valuable for anyone involved in online education and teaching."

—James Riley Estep Jr., professor of Christian education at Lincoln Christian University

"*Teaching the World* is a worthy read for theological educators contemplating the biblical legitimacy, contemporary value, and effective best practices of online theological education. Cartwright, Etzel, Jackson, and Jones challenge us to think not merely of the pragmatic advantages of online education but to examine biblical precedence for its use in accomplishing the vital task of ministerial training. This book furthers the discussion on the integration between theology and educational theory. Highlights of this work include the necessity of spiritual formation online, best practices for online theological education, and leveraging the ministry context of the online learner."

—Kristen Ferguson, director of online education, Gateway Seminary

"This work is essential reading for anyone interested in the theory and practice of online ministerial education. The authors effectively use the apostle Paul's epistolary practice and contemporary social presence theory to propose theological foundations for online theological education. They offer theologically informed best practices for hiring and development of online faculty and effective use of the online classroom. Most helpfully, they focus on the goal of spiritual formation and stress the importance of connecting online learning to students' lived context in their face to face faith communities."

—John L. Gresham, professor of systematic theology, Kenrick-Glennon Seminary

"Traditional forms of theological education are changing with the rise of distant education, particularly online education. The primary criticism of online education is the lack of human embodiment for personal and spiritual formation. *Teaching the World* provides a historical and biblical framework to consider how online education can be an effective means of ministry formation. It also provides research about how to design and develop online courses for effective learning. This book is a helpful resource for faculty and administrators as they seek proven and effective online educational practices."

— Mark A. Maddix, dean, School of Theology & Christian Ministry, and professor of practical theology, Point Loma Nazarene University

"Mind-stretching, that's *Teaching the World*. Assessing the pros and cons of online learning for higher theological education, the authors' balanced approach is a must-read for seminary administrators and faculties. I also commend it to parish pastors. If you'll bridge the book's insights to your congregation, you'll teach more effectively and reach beyond the walls of your Sunday sanctuary. I'll be sharing *Teaching the World* with many colleagues."

— Dale A. Meyer, president, Concordia Seminary

TEACHING
THE WORLD

TEACHING THE WORLD

Foundations for Online Theological Education

TIMOTHY PAUL JONES, JOHN CARTWRIGHT,
GABRIEL ETZEL, AND CHRISTOPHER JACKSON

FOREWORD BY DAVID S. DOCKERY

NASHVILLE, TENNESSEE

Teaching the World
Copyright © 2017 by John Cartwright, Gabriel Etzel,
Christopher D. Jackson, and Timothy Paul Jones

Published by B&H Academic
Nashville, Tennessee

All rights reserved.

ISBN: 978-1-4336-9159-1 (print)

Dewey Decimal Classification: 230.071
Subject Heading: CHRISTIAN COLLEGES AND UNIVERSITIES \
INTERNET IN EDUCATION \ CHRISTIAN EDUCATION–CURRICULA

Unless otherwise noted, all Scripture is from The ESV® Bible (The Holy Bible, English Standard Version®). ESV® Permanent Text Edition® (2016). Copyright © 2001 by Crossway, a publishing ministry of Good News Publishers. All rights reserved.

Scripture quotations marked CSB have been taken from the Christian Standard Bible®, Copyright © 2017 by Holman Bible Publishers. Used by permission. Christian Standard Bible® and CSB® are federally registered trademarks of Holman Bible Publishers.

The web addresses referenced in this book were live and correct at the time of the book's publication but may be subject to change.

First printing: 2017

Printed in the United States of America

Contents

Foreword   xi
Preface   xv
Acknowledgments   xvii

Chapter 1: Past Patterns and Present Challenges in Online Theological Education   1

Section I: Better Foundations for Online Learning   15

Chapter 2: Paul and the Possibility of Absent Presence   21

Chapter 3: Social Presence and Theological Education   37

Chapter 4: Controversy and Common Ground   53

Section II: Better Faculty for Online Learning   67

Chapter 5: Online Faculty and the Image of God   71

Chapter 6: Online Faculty and Theological Competency   89

Chapter 7: Shaping the Spiritual Lives of Online Faculty   107

Section III: Better Practices in the Classroom   131

Chapter 8: Best Practices for Online Learning   137

Chapter 9: Best Practices for Online Ministry Training   153

Chapter 10: The Advantage of Ministry Training in Context   169

Conclusion: To Teach, to Delight, and to Persuade   183
Subject Index   187

Foreword

Theological educators in the twenty-first century have been asking key questions regarding educational philosophy, methodology, and delivery system possibilities. How to navigate these issues and trends has become a complex challenge for many. Much wisdom is needed to think about these challenges in light of more traditional approaches to theological education, in light of recent cultural and education trends, in light of the issues associated with the need for efficient budget models, and in light of the importance for a thoughtful response to expanding global opportunities. These matters continue to swirl and to expand in number and complexity, most of which can be summarized in terms of technology, delivery systems, the interface between tradition and trends, and the need to rethink traditional classroom boundaries. To understand the creative proposals offered in the new volume that you hold in your hands, it will be helpful to understand how traditional theological education has developed through the centuries.[1]

The Development of Theological Education

Theological institutions have a responsibility to prepare ministers for the opportunities they will encounter in their service to the churches,

---

1 See David S. Dockery, "Theological Education Handbook: An Introduction," in *Theology, Church, and Ministry: A Handbook for Theological Education*, ed. David S. Dockery (Nashville: B&H, 2017); also, see Justo L. González, *The History of Theological Education* (Nashville: Abingdon, 2015).

in the culture and for the world. Much of this preparation is focused on the classical disciplines of theology in order for students to be thoroughly grounded in the teachings of Scripture and theology. In the early church, little difference can be discerned between the theological preparation provided for church members and that designed for other church leaders. Pastors and church leaders were called to ongoing study (2 Tim 2:15) in order to provide oversight for the ministry of the Word of God in the midst of worship services, as well as to train and disciple new converts (2 Tim 2:2; Titus 1:9). Formal training during the second and third centuries expanded through the influence of Justin Martyr, Irenaeus, Tertullian, and Origen.

The imprint of Athanasius and Augustine shaped the fourth and fifth centuries. Augustine's influence on theological education has been incalculable. Some even suggest that the development of the theological tradition over the past fifteen hundred years can best be understood as a footnote to the work of Augustine, including his personal mentoring, guidance, and teaching of pastors and bishops. Augustine's work continues to be an important resource for theological education.

Theological education during the medieval period was challenged, expanded, and strengthened through the efforts of Anselm, Bernard of Clairvaux, and Thomas Aquinas. The aims of medieval institutions, however, were not focused on ministerial preparation so much as philosophical and contemplative inquiry. As significant as was the work that took place in the medieval universities, it was the pivotal work of the leading Reformers in the sixteenth century that influenced ministerial preparation as practiced today in most evangelical contexts. Moreover, it was Philip Melanchthon, who more than anyone else in the Reformation period, advanced theological education initiatives.

Melanchthon proposed a new theological curriculum that emphasized the study of Scripture in the original languages. He proposed beginning with the study of Romans, then moving to the rest of the New Testament, then to the Old Testament, and concluding with the study of the Gospel of John. The study of theology began with the study of God, moving to the doctrines of creation, sin, redemption, law and gospel, concluding with eschatology. From this period came the threefold aspects of the curriculum that have influenced the shape of theological education for nearly five centuries: (1) the study of the

Bible and its interpretation, (2) the study of doctrinal theology, and (3) the application of these subjects with special attention to the practical administration of churches, preaching, worship, and ministry. Formal theological studies became a requirement for ministerial ordination during the sixteenth century.

Theological Education for a Rapidly Changing World

Building on the developments in and shaping influences on theological education, Timothy Paul Jones, Christopher Jackson, Gabriel Etzel, and John Cartwright have put forth a vision for a wise and thoughtful approach for the delivery of theological education that includes a commitment to the intentional formation of God-called men and women for the faithful practice of ministry among persons who are collectively the beloved bride of Christ. Recognizing that intentional formation for ministry requires personal care and interaction, our authors have proposed a winsome and constructive path forward.[2]

Jones, Jackson, Etzel, and Cartwright have persuasively offered a creative proposal for offering quality online theological education by developing faculty in an intentional manner that will result in better practices for the classroom. Recognizing that many theological educators remain unconvinced regarding the value of online education, our authors have given us a well-conceived plan worthy of serious consideration. The motivation and vision for the authors' proposal described by the book's title, *Teaching the World*, is grounded in the Great Commission itself and the words of Jesus calling his followers to make disciples of all the nations (Matt 28:18–20).

It should not go unnoticed that the proposal put forth in this volume developed within the context of The Southern Baptist Theological Seminary, a context that has opened doors and pioneered numerous earlier initiatives in theological education.[3] The numerous groundbreaking initiatives that have developed in this context over the past

2   See Kevin J. Vanhoozer and Owen Strachan, *The Pastor as Public Theologian* (Grand Rapids: Baker, 2015), 183–88.
3   See Gregory A. Wills, *Southern Baptist Theological Seminary 1859–2009* (Oxford: Oxford University Press, 2009); also David S. Dockery, "Southern Seminary and the Theological Heritage of Southern Baptists," *The Southern Seminary Magazine* 63, no. 2 (1995): 2–5.

150 years have provided opportunity for enlargement in the subject matter to be taught, increased the number of electives for students, addressed developing needs in multi-staff churches, and opened doors for advanced graduate study. This fertile context shaped the opportunity for the creative proposal offered by Jones, Jackson, Etzel, and Cartwright in this new volume.

Regardless of what one may think about the value of online education, theological educators are in agreement that the future of theological education must prioritize commitments to both intercultural and international initiatives.[4] In that regard, *Teaching the World* offers a helpful, hopeful, insightful, and balanced perspective, offering guidance for the future with careful warnings against wrongheaded fads. I join with the authors of this book in praying that the faithful understandings and commitments herein presented will help ensure the quality work of theological educators who are dedicated to the preparation of the next generation of ministers for service to and in the church of the Lord Jesus Christ.[5]

—David S. Dockery
President, Trinity Evangelical Divinity School

---

[4] See Timothy C. Tennent, *Theology in the Context of World Christianity* (Grand Rapids: Zondervan, 2007); see also David S. Dockery, *Renewing Minds: Serving Church and Society through Christian Higher Education* (Nashville: B&H, 2008), 138–49.

[5] See Daniel L. Akin, ed., *Theology for the Church* (Nashville: B&H, 2014).

Preface

The genesis of this book can be traced to meetings with three doctoral students, each one seeking a topic for his capstone project. At that time, I had been recently appointed as associate vice president over online learning at The Southern Baptist Theological Seminary, and each of these students had an interest in more effective pedagogical practices. Two of my students were also educational administrators. What all of us recognized individually is that many Christian educational institutions seemed to be leaping headlong into online education for purely pragmatic reasons. Together we saw the deep need for theologically grounded online programs in Christian educational institutions. Each student determined to develop as his capstone project a different aspect of these missing theological foundations. Now, these students' research has been sharpened and combined with my own research to form *Teaching the World*, a book that reframes online learning by looking at distance education through a sharply focused theological lens. Although the focus is on training for vocational ministry, this volume will be helpful for any educational institution that wants its theological commitments to shape the design and delivery of online courses.

To help readers to develop plans for online learning in their particular contexts, Christopher Jackson has addressed theological criticisms of online learning, with the goal of developing biblical and theological principles that will both limit and sustain online theological education. Gabriel Etzel has examined faculty recruitment and training from the perspective of theological anthropology. John Cartwright's focus has been on practical pedagogy, demonstrating how the intentional connection of content to the student's context is one key to effective online ministry training.

Each contributor recognizes the value of face-to-face preparation for ministry, as well as the unfortunate truth that some institutions seem to be pursuing online programs for purely pragmatic reasons. At the same time, we believe that there are ways to develop online ministry training programs that refuse to compromise theological content or ministerial preparation. To do this, we cannot simply convert on-campus content into an online experience that includes everything except the shared space of a physical campus. Online programs in Christian institutions must be designed in fundamentally distinct ways that are shaped by Scripture and by our theological confessions. The content of each course should be linked to the student's context and should facilitate the formation of face-to-face community wherever the student lives. It is our prayer that this book will equip professors and administrators in Christian educational institutions throughout the world to think more theologically about online learning so that Christ may be more glorified in the ministers we train to lead his church.

—Timothy Paul Jones
Associate Vice President for the Global Campus
The Southern Baptist Theological Seminary

Acknowledgments

John Cartwright: I am thankful to God for his grace with regard to this writing opportunity. I am grateful to my writing companions and colleagues in this project. Additionally, I want to thank Liberty University for the opportunity to be a part of the exciting and ever-changing landscape of online education. I am also thankful to B&H for their confidence in the need for this book and for shepherding this book from concept to completion. Finally, I am thankful to my wife, Kristen, and her longsuffering during those long hours of writing!

Gabriel Etzel: I am extremely grateful for the investment others have made in my life that make these projects possible. Thank you to the other authors of this text, to my colleagues and to the academic leadership at Liberty University, to my fellow students and professors at The Southern Baptist Theological Seminary, and to my wife and children. You have each blessed my life beyond measure.

Christopher Jackson: Many thanks to all those who helped make this work a reality. These include the Lexington Public Library, Lexington Theological Seminary library, Concordia Seminary, Saint Louis library, The Southern Baptist Theological Seminary library, Concordia University Wisconsin library, Wisconsin Lutheran Seminary library, Nashotah House Theological Seminary library, my research partners John Cartwright and Gabriel Etzel, Betsy Fredrick for editing assistance, Dr. Timothy Jones for guidance, and—above all—my wife, Mary.

Timothy Paul Jones: This book would not have been possible apart from the joyous journey that I have shared with these three doctoral students, the manifold support that I have received from the administration of The Southern Baptist Theological Seminary, and the encouragement of my wife and three daughters. Thanks are also due to Michael Graham for his work on the subject index. To God be the glory for each of these unmerited blessings.

CHAPTER 1

Past Patterns and Present Challenges in Online Theological Education

I have never been a traditional college student.
I have earned three degrees but never once lived on a college or seminary campus. While earning every one of my degrees, I have worked forty hours a week or more. In the process, I have witnessed a momentous shift in higher education—a movement from traditional, on-campus education in fall and spring semesters to an increasingly complex mixture of online and on-campus components scattered across the calendar. Now, I am privileged to lead the global campus at one of the largest seminaries in the world and to oversee the research of doctoral students in the field of online learning.

My circuitous pathway to this position began with a badly bungled telephone call.

The Great College Catalog Confusion

Sometime in my early teenage years, I discovered that everything I had any interest in doing—law, military history, and political science were piquing my interest at the time—would require a college degree.

Halfway through high school, it occurred to me that I might need to find out more about what was required to go to college. Neither of my parents had finished high school, and no one in my family had ever earned a college degree; so, even though my parents encouraged me every step of the way, they didn't know precisely how to guide me. The high school I attended was a tiny fundamentalist academy where the faculty's only qualifications were certificates from unaccredited Bible institutes; so they weren't much help when it came to an accredited college education.

In the summer between my sophomore and junior years of high school, I went to the library, located the toll-free telephone numbers for a handful of colleges, and began making calls. I don't recall which college I called first, but I do recall the awkward conversation that followed. As soon as someone answered the telephone, I announced, "I need to know how people go to your college"—because I didn't know what else to say.

"Well, if you'll provide me with your address, I'll be glad to send you a college catalog," said the young woman on the other end of the line.

When I heard the word "catalog," what crossed my mind were the only catalogs I knew—department store catalogs, filled with products for sale—and I was certain she'd misunderstood what I needed.

"I don't want to buy anything," I replied. "I just need to know how to take classes so I can get a college degree."

"If you'll give me your address, I'll send a catalog so you can do that," she repeated.

After a couple more confused exchanges, I finally gave her my address, reasoning that I could simply throw their catalog in the trash once it arrived. A few days later, I was surprised to discover that a college catalog wasn't a colorful magazine filled with products for sale at all. It was exactly what I needed to figure out how to earn a college degree—a small book that explained the college's degree programs, tuition rates, and scholarships.

By the time I graduated from high school, I had sensed a calling to vocational ministry, and my resolve to find a way to earn a college degree was stronger than ever. My ACT scores had qualified me as a State Scholar, which covered much of my tuition, and our household's finances made me eligible for an educational opportunity grant for low-income families. Still, I didn't have the resources to cover room and board in addition to the cost of tuition and books. And so, I lived at home—about a half-hour drive from campus—and I worked one part-time job at the library and another part-time job at a Christian bookstore, in addition to serving as a worship minister on weekends. I couldn't always fit the courses I needed around my work schedule. The college I attended didn't offer summer or winter sessions, so I took three or four correspondence courses every summer from another college. Each of these courses came with a syllabus, sometimes supplemented with audiocassette tapes, and a list of textbooks. I completed the assignments and mailed them to a teacher with a self-addressed stamped envelope. A few weeks after sending off each assignment, I received my graded work back in the mail.

One of my tasks in my part-time job at the library was assigning call numbers to new books and cataloging them. Near the end of my first year as a college student, a new step was added to the process. I would verify the accuracy of each call number by accessing records at the Library of Congress through a computer connected to a network known (if I recall correctly) as UUNET AlterNet. I saw nothing but text on a blue screen, but I was in awe. Here I was, in a library in Kansas, looking directly at records that were located in Washington, D.C. Little did I know that this same technology was already in the process of revolutionizing education in a way that would change the future direction of my life.

A Better Way to Do This

During my last summer of college, a small-town church in Missouri called me as their pastor, and I moved into a parsonage next door to the church building. By this time, I had concluded that I needed seminary training—but the nearest seminary to my church was nearly two hours away. At this particular seminary, no courses were available via distance education, and no classes were offered in any format other than four days per week. Once again, I found myself driving back and forth to get an education—except that I was now driving almost four hours each day, four days per week. Meanwhile, a congregation of believers in a small town was looking to me for leadership and pastoral care.

I tried to make the best of those hours in the car, listening to audiocassettes of the Scriptures and to lecture series from Ligonier Ministries. Sometimes I spent a night or two in Kansas City instead of making the long haul home. Yet, the fact that I was missing from the church most of the week took a toll on my effectiveness as a pastor. Over and over during those many long hours on the highway, I found myself thinking, *Surely, there's a better way to do this.*

Three years after graduating from seminary, I found myself longing to complete a research doctorate, and it was my quest for a doctoral program that opened the door to experiencing a "better way." By this time, I was serving a church in Oklahoma, far away from any opportunity to complete a doctorate in any subject matter in which I was interested. During my first year in that church, I learned about a new doctoral program at The Southern Baptist Theological Seminary. Dial-up Internet was available almost everywhere in the United States by this point, and Southern Seminary was experimenting with doctoral courses that blended Internet-based discussions with on-campus seminars that were packed into intensive one-week and two-week formats. Students pursued their degrees in cohorts and completed their coursework together. Now, instead of making dozens of trips to campus every semester, I made only three trips per year.

When I was on campus in Louisville, I was able to spend focused time researching and writing with a community of fellow doctoral students. When I was at home in Oklahoma, I interacted with my cohort and our professors in online discussion forums. There we wrestled with content that we were reading and related our readings to our ministry contexts. This was by far the most enriching educational experience of my life—but it was possible only because of an explosive growth in online learning in the closing years of the twentieth century.

The goal of this book is to respond to the growth of online learning over the past couple of decades in ways that are biblically and theologically grounded, particularly when it comes to the ways that we prepare men and women to become leaders in the church. Our intent is to steer a clear path between an uncritical embrace of online theological education on the one hand and a complete rejection of this pedagogical modality on the other. First, however, let's lay a foundation for our study by taking a brief look together at the history of distance education, with a focus on theological education.[1]

The Development of Distance Education

I have organized the history of distance education into four phases. You will quickly notice, though, that these phases haven't started or ended at precise points in time in history. Each one overlaps with others, revealing the rapidly shifting approaches that have marked distance education over the past three centuries.

Distance Education

Education of students who are not physically present with the instructor.

The First Phase of Distance Education: Print and Postal Service (1700s–1990s)

At least one historian of distance education has suggested that the apostle Paul may have been an early distance educator, if distance education is understood as teaching without being physically present.[2] Although—as you will see in the first part of this book—there are connections to be made between Paul's epistles and distance education, such a complete correlation seems to me to be too much of a stretch. I suggest that the first era of distance education as we know it began with the correspondence courses of the eighteenth and nineteenth centuries. The earliest surviving evidence of a correspondence course seems to be this notice in the *Boston Gazette*, dated March 20, 1728:

> Caleb Phillipps, Teacher of the new method of Short Hand claims that "Persons in the Country desirous to Learn this Art, may by having the several Lessons sent Weekly to them, be as perfectly instructed as those that live in Boston."[3]

---

1 For a comprehensive survey of sources and gaps in the history of distance education, see Von V. Pittman, "University Correspondence Study," in *Handbook of Distance Education*, ed. M. G. Moore (New York: Routledge, 2013), 21–36.
2 Börje Holmberg, *The Evolution, Principles and Practices of Distance Education* (Oldenburg: Bibliotheks- und Informationssystem der Universität, 2005), 13.
3 Ibid. See also Holmberg's work, *Growth and Structure of Distance Education* (London; Wolfeboro, NH: Croom Helm, 1986), 6.

Face-to-face instruction was the standard of comparison in this little advertisement ("as perfectly instructed as those that live in Boston"), and there seems to have been some skepticism regarding whether Phillipps's correspondence course could produce the same results as face-to-face instruction ("claims that [they] may . . . be as perfectly instructed"). Like a quality online instructor today, Phillipps made consistent contact with his students and organized his materials into manageable chunks ("by having the several Lessons sent Weekly").

By the mid-nineteenth century, the inventor of the Pitman system of shorthand was using "Penny Postcards" to offer similar correspondence courses in England.[4] In the closing decades of the nineteenth century, an American professor named William Rainey Harper offered what may have been the first graduate-level theological course in a distance format. At the Baptist Union Theological Seminary in Illinois, Harper experimented with teaching Hebrew via correspondence. The results of his experiments were mixed, but the primary impact of Harper's efforts would be realized later, on the shores of Chautauqua Lake in New York and through the birth of a new university in Chicago.[5]

During the summers, Harper taught at the Chautauqua Lake Sunday School Assembly. The founding vision of Chautauqua was that "education, once the peculiar privilege of the few . . . , [would] become the valued possession of the many."[6] Already having experimented with correspondence courses as a professor, Harper became instrumental in the early leadership of a correspondence program at Chautauqua known as the Literary and Scientific Circle.[7] Soon a School of Theology had emerged at Chautauqua as well. By 1883, Chautauqua

---

[4] Alfred Baker, *The Life of Sir Isaac Pitman* (London: I. Pitman & Sons, Ltd., 1908), 182–83.

[5] Michael G. Moore and Greg Kearsley, *Distance Education: A Systems View of Online Learning*, 3rd ed. (Belmont, CA: Wadsworth Cengage Learning, 2012), 25.

[6] John Heyl Vincent, *The Chautauqua Movement* (Boston: Chautauqua Press, 1886), 2.

[7] John C. Scott, "The Chautauqua Movement: Revolution in Popular Higher Education," *The Journal of Higher Education* 70, no. 4 (1999): 389–412, doi:10.2307/2649308.

was a state-chartered university, offering the first distance-education degrees in the United States.⁸

In 1892, Harper became the inaugural president of the University of Chicago, and Chautauqua began to phase out its external degree programs.⁹ At the University of Chicago, Harper initiated the first university-based program of distance education.¹⁰ Still, even as Harper promoted correspondence courses, he never saw correspondence courses as a replacement for "oral instruction." Instead, he argued that distance education should remain organically related to a physical institution of research and higher education where face-to-face instruction occurred.¹¹

In the opening years of the twentieth century, Moody Bible Institute followed a pattern of distance education similar to the one that Harper had already established a few miles south at the University of Chicago. Moody's Correspondence Department provided theological education for laypeople as well as church leaders "who have not the time or means to take a college or seminary education."¹² Their rationale reveals much about perceptions of distance education in the late nineteenth and early twentieth centuries:

> There is a crying need for competent Bible teachers, and also for those who understand the Word of God and know how to use it in bringing others to Christ. . . . [The] Correspondence Department has been organized for the benefit of those of both sexes who cannot, for financial or other reasons, attend the Institute personally. . . .
>
> For more than twenty years correspondence schools have been in existence. Several of these are of large proportions. Almost every conceivable subject is being taught, not only languages and

---

8   John E. Tapia, *Circuit Chautauqua: From Rural Education to Popular Entertainment in Early Twentieth Century America* (Jefferson, NC: McFarland & Co., 1997), 22.
9   Von Pittman, "An Alien Presence," *American Educational History* 35 (2008): 170.
10 Moore and Kearsley, *Distance Education*, 25.
11 Jack D. Dilbeck, "Perceptions of Academic Administrators towards Quality Indicators in Internet Based Distance Education" (Ph.D. diss., Indiana State University, 2008), 17–18, http://search.proquest.com/docview/304608510/abstract.
12 *The Institute Tie* (Chicago: Moody Bible Institute, 1900), 105.

literary departments of knowledge, but also scientific and practical subjects, such as civil and mechanical engineering, architecture, electricity, chemistry, etc. Education by correspondence is no longer an experiment. Not only is teaching by correspondence possible and practicable, but it has many advantages.

1. It is available for any man or woman who lives within reach of the mails. Distance is no barrier.
2. Studies do not interfere with daily duties.
3. There are no limitations as to age, sex, or race.
4. Each student is a personal pupil, coming under the direct, personal care of the teacher.
5. Studies are always ready and available.
6. Students can begin or drop study any time to suit their own convenience.
7. Each student sets his or her own pace. . . .

Each course is taken up in sections, printed in pamphlets containing 40 to 60 pages, which can be conveniently carried in the pocket for study on train, street car, while lunching, or whenever time can be spared.[13]

In the year 1900 no less than today, distance education was promoted as an accessible and affordable alternative for those who were unable to relocate to a physical campus. Correspondence training was already accepted in a range of technical disciplines. Moody Bible Institute seems to have borrowed its model of education from these disciplines, quite possibly as practiced at the nearby University of Chicago, and applied it to training for ministry.[14]

---

13 Ibid., 105–6.
14 A valid question worth asking at this point has to do with whether ministry preparation is more skill development or character formation. The advertisement from the Moody Correspondence Department seems to suggest that ministry training may be pursued like "scientific and practical subjects, such as civil and mechanical engineering, architecture, electricity, chemistry." If ministry preparation is more character formation than skill development, however (and I believe that it is), preparation from a distance requires far more than impartation of information or the attainment of particular skills. However difficult it may be, ministry preparation requires some measure of formation in the context of face-to-face community.

The Second Phase of Distance Education: Print Supplemented by Multiple Media (1920s–2000s)

The second phase of distance education began when educational organizations began to supplement printed correspondence courses with other media. Radio, records, films, audiocassettes, compact discs, television programs, and eventually videocassettes and digital videodiscs buttressed the print content of correspondence courses. By the 1980s, Coastline Community College was broadcasting telecourses that led to college degrees, and Nova Southeastern University was beginning to offer computer-based graduate courses.

In Christian contexts, many of these courses were aimed at personal enrichment and the training of laypeople, much like Moody's Correspondence Department earlier in the twentieth century. In 1975, R. C. Sproul and Ligonier Ministries released their first series of audiocassettes, some of which made seminary-level content available to laypeople. The next year, Liberty Baptist College launched non-accredited training through the Liberty Home Bible Institute. Liberty took its first steps toward accredited distance education in 1985, offering courses for academic credit through the Liberty University School of Lifelong Learning. On-campus lectures were videotaped and mailed to students, who completed the same coursework as on-campus students and mailed assignments back to the university.

The Third Phase of Distance Education: Online Learning Supplemented by Other Media (1980s–2010s)

As Internet access began to penetrate millions of homes in the closing decades of the twentieth century, institutions that were already offering distance education courses moved rapidly into a new transitional phase of distance education. In this third phase, a computer connected to the Internet coexisted alongside other media; students in this transitional era frequently watched their lectures on videotapes or DVDs, but they also submitted assignments and interacted with professors and fellow students via email or discussion forums.

The Fourth Phase of Distance Education: Multiple Media Delivered Online (1990s–Present)

With the increasing speed and accessibility of the Internet, a fourth era in distance education quickly eclipsed the third. In this fourth phase, every aspect of the course—videos and syllabi from the faculty, finished assignments from the students, discussions and group projects shared among students—began to be delivered online. When the Association of Theological Schools (ATS) issued a clear decision about online courses in the year 2000, their initial approach was radical limitation. Even after limited online courses were permitted, master of divinity students in ATS-accredited schools were required to complete at least one-third of their degrees on campus. In 2012, the ATS Board of Commissioners made the momentous decision to grant exceptions to the on-campus requirement.[15] Already more than a dozen ATS-accredited seminaries are offering fully online master of divinity degrees, with many more petitions in preparation.

The Problem and the Promise of Online Training for Ministry

Perspectives vary widely on whether online courses are a suitable medium for the training of God-called ministers. Some have suggested that "online discussion forums are a perfect opportunity for seminarians to realize that the knowledge they are acquiring is meant to be shared, and the forums themselves provide them with the venue in which to practice skills of communication related to the evangelization of others."[16] Others have taken the opposite perspective, declaring that "online education for credit does not *aid*, much less *enrich*, theological education. It dehumanizes it. It takes us too far from a biblical pattern of theological education."[17]

My perspective is somewhere in between. I'm thankful for the flexibility that online education has made possible. I know from past

---

15 "Fully-Online-Degree-Programs.pdf," 1, accessed January 8, 2016, http://www.ats.edu/uploads/resources/publications-presentations/documents/fully-online-degree-programs.pdf.
16 Sebastian Mahfood and Paule Barbeau, "Considering Human and Spiritual Formation in Distance Learning," *Colloquy* (Spring 2012): 34.
17 Paul House, "Hewing to Scripture's Pattern," *Colloquy* (Spring 2010): 4.

experience the deep struggle of desiring an education but never having the financial resources to quit work and move to a campus. Today I am privileged to work with students from around the globe in online courses, facilitating their assimilation of new knowledge. Right now, in one online course with about twenty students, I'm teaching ministers scattered across twelve different states and three different continents, and I have one student whose location I don't even know because he's serving in a country that's closed to the gospel.

At the same time, I'm also cautious about training pastors and other ministers from a distance. I have no doubt that online education can produce the same test scores as on-campus education.[18] Yet, preparation for ministry is far more than a mere movement of data from the professor's mind to a student's memory. Ministry preparation requires the intentional formation of God-called men and women for the faithful practice of ministry among persons who are collectively the beloved bride of Christ. Intentional formation for ministry requires personal care and interaction.

As I watch the rapid growth of online learning, my most pressing concern is that theological seminaries may transition their training to online formats for purely pragmatic reasons—recruitment, retention, and the pursuit of profitability. What can quickly be forgotten in this rush toward online education is that the Scriptures and our theological confessions should shape not only the content of our courses but also their design and delivery. If the Scriptures and our theological confessions don't determine the design and delivery of courses, preparation for ministry will be reduced from the pursuit of Christ-centered formation to a bare transfer of theological information.

---

18 In my own institution, examinations and papers from online students are consistently compared with the work of on-campus students by having faculty grade a group of assignments from a multiplicity of course formats. Faculty are unaware of which assignments were completed by online or on-campus students. The grades given to assignments from online students have never differed significantly from grades given to assignments from on-campus students. Other studies have reported similar findings. See, e.g., Anna Ya Ni, "Comparing the Effectiveness of Classroom and Online Learning," *Journal of Public Affairs Education* 19 (2013): 199, 212; Steven Stack, "Learning Outcomes in an Online versus Traditional Course," *International Journal for the Scholarship of Teaching and Learning* 9 (2015): article 5.

Looking at the landscape of theological education in my own institution and elsewhere with these concerns in mind, I find myself repeatedly returning to three key questions:

(1) *How will we teach students to value place if students and faculty are never together in the same place?* The locations where we live and serve, eat and play, foster friendships and form families are not holding tanks where we await the cosmic salvation of our spirits. These locations are pregnant with rhythms of life and relationships that reflect the splendor of humanity's creation in God's image. God did not design us to live as disembodied avatars in virtual worlds but as bundles of bone and flesh and soul interwoven in place and space. Particularly for pastors in training, it is essential to develop the discipline of learning the story of a particular place and participating deeply in the life of that place. When seminary faculty and students live and learn together in the same location, their shared love for that location cultivates the students' capacity to value the locales where they will serve in the future. In online learning, faculty and institutions are faced with the far more difficult task of simultaneously shaping the student's love for his or her own context and for the seminary community when the two contexts may never overlap. If a student never values the seminary as a community woven in time and place, the institution will be perceived as nothing more than an educational vending machine from which the student receives a credential after inserting the appropriate amounts of cash and effort. The degree serves not as a marker of the student's formation for ministry but as a commodity that's necessary for professional advancement. Merely living in the same location doesn't guarantee a student's formation by the faculty, of course—but living apart makes such formation more difficult and more complex. Online seminary education must be designed and delivered so that students simultaneously develop deep appreciation for the institution and deep love for the places where God has called them to serve.

(2) *How will we select, value, and equip faculty for a task that requires more time and engagement than an on-campus class?* In an on-campus course, a student gleans much information informally through a professor's unscripted digressions in class, in comments overheard in hallways, and through conversations with fellow students in the café. Online student can't pick up this informal information as easily as on-campus

students. The result is that online learning requires greater effort and engagement from the faculty than on-campus education, which in turn calls for smaller class sizes and more faculty. Furthermore, in some instances, an online course may be developed using an on-campus professor's video content and then delivered to students under the guidance of an adjunct instructor. If these adjunct instructors are under-compensated or under-equipped, such a system exploits the instructors and provides students with subpar education. However, when adjuncts are highly trained and highly valued, they can provide an equivalent or even superior experience for students—especially in theological education, where many of these adjuncts are active and faithful pastors with research doctorates. Effective online theological education requires a corps of well-compensated and well-equipped adjunct faculty, who are appropriately credentialed and actively engaged in ministry.

(3) *How will we effectively partner with the student's local church so that this congregation becomes the student's primary context for formation as a minister?* Many expressions of online learning focus on the development of virtual learning communities in online environments. Online discussion forums and video chats are helpful pedagogical practices that should certainly be part of every online course design. And yet, I'm increasingly convinced that the assumption that such tools can provide a platform for the formation of authentic community may be misguided. Fellowship is primarily physical and face-to-face, and God has designed the local church to fulfill this purpose in the lives of his people. When it comes to ministers in training, perhaps the primary locus of the online student's community of learning should be his or her local church.[19] What this would mean practically is that projects conducted in the student's local church would become an essential part of the curriculum. More important, it would require leaders in the local church to provide guidance for the student and feedback for

---

19 This suggestion stands in respectful contrast to the perspective presented, e.g., in Joanne Jung, *Character Formation in Online Education* (Grand Rapids: Zondervan, 2015). While agreeing wholeheartedly with Jung's call for online instructors to lead students to character formation through presence and inspiration, formation of students for ministry requires a distinct centeredness in the local church that does not necessarily characterize Jung's approach.

the professor, so that the congregation joins forces with the seminary to create a thriving context for the student's ministry formation.

These are the questions that Christopher Jackson, Gabriel Etzel, and John Cartwright explore throughout this book. The result will be a vision for online theological education that grounds students in particular places, that equips faculty for spiritual formation, and that elevates the role of the local church in ministry training. These values are already shaping the institution that I serve, and my hope is that they will soon begin to shape yours as well.

Opportunities for Application

Discover

1. Analyze the reasons for implementing online education in one's institution.
2. Analyze the limitations placed on online education in one's institution.

Decide

1. Determine to equip students to value place and to see the local church as a primary context for their training as ministers.
2. Determine to value adjunct instructors and to seek equitable compensation for them.

Do

1. Evaluate institutional policies related to adjunct instructors, looking for areas where adjunct instructors are devalued or treated inequitably.
2. Implement faculty training that emphasizes the importance of place and the centrality of the local church.

Section I
Better Foundations for Online Learning

How the Pauline Epistles and Contemporary Social Presence Theory Offer Guidance for Online Learning

Over the past few decades a debate has arisen concerning the appropriateness of using online formats for theological education. Some believe that online formats can be beneficial for theological education. Others believe that these formats are inappropriate for theological education. The participants in the debate have usually argued from different categories and with different concerns; real communication has therefore seldom occurred. In particular, those who are optimistic about online theological education tend to justify it by appealing to pragmatic benefits. They may argue that online formats will open theological education up to a broader student population or that these formats will allow students to remain in their particular ministry contexts while pursuing education.[1] In contrast, those who believe that the use of online formats is inappropriate for theological education tend to base their

---

[1] Meri MacLeod, "The Case for Distance Learning in Theological Education: Six Strategic Benefits of Interactive Web-Based Distance Learning," *Colloquy* 18, no. 2 (2010): 7; Van B. Weigel, "Reflection: Place in the Digital Age: Familiar Dichotomies No Longer Apply," *Christian Scholar's Review* 32, no. 1 (2002): 14–18; Stephen Haar, "E-Constructing Theological Education for Ministry in a www World," *Lutheran Theological Journal* 42, no. 1 (May 2008): 18–29; M. E. Hess, "Attending to Embodiedness in Online, Theologically Focused Learning" (paper presented at Going the Distance: Theology, Religious Education, and Interactive Distance Education, University of Dayton, 1999); MacLeod, "The Case for Distance Learning"; Matthew C. Ogilvie, "Teaching Theology Online," *Australian EJournal of Theology* 13, no. 1 (2009): 66.

concerns on theology. They may argue that the fact that Christ took on human flesh indicates that theological education, too, should take place in the flesh, in a face-to-face environment.[2]

Critics of the use of online formats in theological education do indeed need to address the pragmatic concerns of online theological education's proponents. And yet, most proponents of online theological education have often failed to answer legitimate theological concerns from the critics. Perhaps such theological defenses are sparse because few have provided a theological foundation for online theological education in the first place.

The unavoidable reality is that theological institutions are frequently and increasingly using online formats. In 2017, 145 out of 271 of the schools in the Association of Theological Schools (ATS) offered at least six online courses.[3] A recent survey has shown that most chief academic officers at institutions of higher learning believe that "online education is critical to the long-term strategy of [their] institution."[4] Online education is no passing fad; it is here to stay.

Yet, many theological institutions have adopted these formats without appropriate theological reflection. Indeed, practical concerns, not theology, have tended to drive the adoption of and implementation of online formats by theological institutions.[5] In other words, external

[2] Steve Delamarter, "Theological Educators and Their Concerns about Technology," *Teaching Theology & Religion* 8, no. 3 (2005): 138, doi:10.1111/j.1467-9647.2005.00237.x; David Diekema and David Caddell, "The Significance of Place: Sociological Reflections on Distance Learning and Christian Higher Education," *Christian Scholar's Review* 31, no. 2 (2001): 182; Paul R. House, "Hewing to Scripture's Pattern: A Plea for Personal Theological Education," *Colloquy* 18, no. 2 (2010): 2, 6.

[3] The Association of Theological Schools, "Member Schools," accessed May 30, 2017, http://www.ats.edu/member-schools; idem, "Schools Offering Six or More Courses Online," accessed May 30, 2017, http://www.ats.edu/member-schools/member-school-distance-education.

[4] I. Elaine Allen and Jeff Seaman, "Going the Distance: Online Education in the United States, 2011," Babson Survey Research Group, November 2011, 8, accessed September 19, 2012, http://www.onlinelearningsurvey.com/reports/goingthedistance.pdf.

[5] For an overview of the pragmatic concerns that have informed the adoption of online formats, see Christopher Dwight Jackson, "The Phenomenon of Social Presence in the Pauline Epistles and Its Implication for Practices of Online Education" (Ed.D. thesis, The Southern Baptist Theological Seminary, 2015), 4–5.

rather than internal factors often motivate the adoption of online education.[6] Internal factors that could drive institutions' choices about online education could include longstanding traditions or theological commitments. Examples of external factors include demands of students and individual churches for online opportunities, financial pressures in institutions, and current trends in education.

These factors should be balanced; but the external ones are often the most immediate and pressing. And thus, these external factors have tended to drive the implementation of online formats in theological education. But adopting online formats simply because of external factors threatens institutional integrity. As the ATS has stated, "Each school must determine the kind of opportunities that are appropriate to its institutional and religious commitment."[7] In other words, the means of instruction must flow from an institution's identity, or from internal factors. It seems, however, that few institutions consider these crucial factors when developing their online programs.

This section looks carefully at this problem, seeking biblical and theological guidance in an area where there has been too little. This exploration will begin by examining Paul's epistolary theory and practice, examining what Paul thought he could accomplish by means of the epistle, making comparisons between Paul's epistolary practice

---

[6] While he does not discuss online education in his article, this "internal vs. external" dichotomy owes to Daniel O. Aleshire: "[Change] will come as a consequence more of external factors than of internal factors. . . . Endowments, tenured faculty members, historically significant buildings, a significant heritage to hold up and live out of—all of these contribute to a kind of internal gradualism. These factors have no influence, however, as soon as you walk off campus. The world around the seminary is not beholden to these factors—often does not even value them—and is much more subject to fundamental shifts, often across very short periods of time. These external shifts form relentless pressures on schools to change." Aleshire, "The Future of Theological Education," 381. One could argue that demand from churches and institutions for online theological education constitutes an internal pressure. Churches and students may demand online formats today, but not tomorrow. Such a demand is not as permanent as doctrine, biblical precedent, or longstanding tradition.

[7] Association of Theological Schools, Preface to the Standards of Accreditation, "Educational Standard and Degree Program Standards" (Association of Theological Schools, 2014), http://www.ats.edu/uploads/accrediting/documents/preface-to-the-standards-of-accreditation.pdf, accessed May 30, 2017.

and online theological education. Chapter 3 will examine Paul's epistolary theory and practice through the lens of contemporary social presence theory. Whereas chapter 2 examines the "what" of Pauline epistolary theory and practice, chapter 3 examines the "how." In other words, chapter 2 discusses what Paul thought the epistle could accomplish in his ministry, and chapter 3 explains how epistles succeeded in such accomplishments. Chapter 3 will conclude by applying these insights to online theological education.

The goal in chapters 2 and 3 is to make judgments and recommendations for online theological education based on Pauline epistolary theory and practice and contemporary social presence theory. Judgments and recommendations will proceed from the evidence. The results of this methodology may be surprising for a book that seeks to serve as a foundation for online theological education. Yes, these chapters will argue that the use of online formats for theological education is legitimate—but this claim will be qualified. Faithful use of online theological education has not only strong potential but also strong limitations. Paul believed that his epistles could accomplish great things, but this was a sober belief that also recognized the drawbacks of conducting ministry by means of the epistle. These chapters will provide a similarly sober perspective on online theological education.

This section will conclude by examining some of the stronger objections against online theological education—as well as some of the less-than-satisfactory responses to these objections—and by explaining how the approach I have proposed offers a better way.

CHAPTER 2

Paul and the Possibility of Absent Presence

This section provides biblical and theological guidance for the adoption of online formats within the field of theological education; the primary means by which it does so is by a comparison to Paul's epistolary theory and practice. This chapter contributes to that goal by exploring Paul's epistolary theory and practice—investigating Paul's opinions regarding the value and purpose of his epistles. However, is such an approach justified? This chapter begins by briefly discussing analogical arguments and the qualities that make for good analogies. Such a discussion will guide the argument as it progresses, and it will also benefit the discussion of chapter 3, which takes up the shortcomings of the analogies of online theological education's strongest detractors.

After this chapter discusses analogies, it will then explore the similarities by which fruitful comparisons between Paul's epistolary theory and practice can be brought to bear on online theological education, and finally it will examine what Paul believed he could accomplish through the epistle.

Analogical Reasoning

Offering theological guidance for online theological education is like making a historic first descent down a river. One cannot rely on set, known routes to dictate the course of navigation. Rather, an explorer must use her past experience to guide her. By floating down rivers the explorer learns that it is typically safer to stay on the inside of a bend, to avoid strong eddy lines, to follow series of waves (a wave train), and to stay out of hydraulic holes, places where the water tumbles vertically over a submerged rock. Following these rules, gained through similar experiences on other rivers, does not yield a safe descent with complete certainty. Avoiding a hydraulic hole may send one toward a dangerous overhanging rock; a wave train may lead over a twenty-foot waterfall. But, in general, the use of previous river experience gives good guidance when descending an unknown river.

A river explorer is using a form of analogical reasoning (albeit a simple form). *The Stanford Encyclopedia of Philosophy* defines an analogy as "a comparison between two objects, or systems of objects, that highlights respects in which they are thought to be similar," and an analogical argument as "an explicit representation of a form of analogical reasoning that cites accepted similarities between two systems to support the conclusion that some further similarity exists."[1] The encyclopedia then goes on to note several functions of analogical reasoning. Analogies often have a heuristic use, serving as "aids to discovery," the use of analogical reasoning to formulating a solution to a new problem being an example of such a heuristic use. They often also play a "justificatory role" in which they can be used to draw some sort of conclusion.

Theological guidance for online theological education must rely on analogical reasoning. Analogical arguments belong to the realm of inductive, as opposed to deductive, logic.[2] That is to say, they are concerned with establishing plausibility, though they do not establish necessity. A good analogical argument, like all good inductive arguments, is a strong argument. The conclusions of the argument are likely, though

---

1 Paul Bartha, "Analogy and Analogical Reasoning," in *The Stanford Encyclopedia of Philosophy*, ed. Edward N. Zalta, Fall 2013, http://plato.stanford.edu/archives/fall2013/entries/reasoning-analogy/.

2 C. Stephen Layman, *The Power of Logic* (Mountain View, CA: Mayfield, 1999), 11–12.

not necessarily, true. For obvious reasons, the Scriptures give no direct guidance regarding online theological education. Theological guidance for online theological education, therefore, will only come by way of comparison. One might say, for example, "Jesus provided theological formation to his disciples in such a way; therefore, this will impact online theological education in such a way as well." This section, both the positive argument that it makes and the criticisms that it makes of other arguments regarding online theological education, relies heavily on analogy and analogical reasoning. Therefore, briefly reviewing the qualities that make for a good analogy will be helpful.

The Stanford Encyclopedia of Philosophy offers these guidelines for evaluating analogical arguments:

> The more similarities (between two domains), the stronger the analogy. . . .
>
> The more differences, the weaker the analogy. . . .
>
> The greater the extent of our ignorance about the two domains, the weaker the analogy. . . .
>
> The weaker the conclusion, the more plausible the analogy.[3]

These guidelines will aid in evaluating the claims made in this section regarding online theological education as well this section's evaluations of the claims of others.

Pauline Epistolary Practice and Online Theological Education

This section makes comparisons between Pauline epistolary theory and practice on the one hand and contemporary online education theory and practice on the other. However, such a comparison is not self-evident, and the epistles and online formats certainly do not correspond perfectly. Thus, this section will begin by first examining the ways in which Pauline epistolary practice is unlike online theological education. Their similarity will then be explored in order to establish a more certain correspondence.

3   Bartha, "Analogy and Analogical Reasoning."

Points of Contrast

The most evident difference between online theological education and Pauline epistolary practice is the medium through which communication occurs. Paul utilizes the letter, a written form of communication. These letters were often carried by emissaries, who would also verbally deliver them to their recipients.[4]

Months could pass until a letter was delivered. While the letter did allow a measure of interaction through mutual correspondence and perhaps through the emissary, such interaction was certainly not immediate by today's standards.[5] On the other hand, online theological education is facilitated mainly through the Internet, and is dependent upon various learning management systems, bulletin boards, social networking sites, and the like. Response time is immediate, and much more back-and-forth interaction occurs.

Another difference is the nature of the educational endeavor. Contemporary theological education is focused on the individual student; whereas, most of Paul's theological content appears in letters to congregations.[6] His letters to individuals, such as the pastoral

---

[4] Ben Witherington, *Paul's Letter to the Romans: A Socio-Rhetorical Commentary* (Grand Rapids: Eerdmans, 2004), 23.

[5] Evidence for interaction between Paul and his congregations is most evident in the Corinthian correspondence. Assuming that the "Severe Letter" mentioned in 2 Corinthians 2:4 and 7:8–11 is now a lost document and not to be identified with 1 Corinthians, then Paul wrote at least three letters to the Corinthians. Victor Paul Furnish, *2 Corinthians,* The Anchor Bible, vol. 32A (Garden City, NY: Doubleday, 1984), 159–160; C. K. Barrett, *The Second Epistle to the Corinthians.* Black's New Testament Commentaries (Peabody, MA: Hendrickson, 1993), 119; Ralph P. Martin, *2 Corinthians,* Word Biblical Commentary, vol. 13 (Waco, TX: Word, 1986), 33. In addition, Paul records multiple reports about the Corinthian congregation (i.e., 1 Cor 1:11 and 2 Cor 7:6–7). A negative report from Corinth is attributed as the reason for the change in tone in 2 Corinthians even by those who hold to the integrity of the letter. Martin, *2 Corinthians,* 298–89. Paul also notes a letter that had come to him from the Corinthians (1 Cor 7:1).

[6] The focus on the individual student is reflected, for example, in ATS's "Degree Program Standards": "The purpose of the Master of Divinity degree is to prepare *persons* for ordained ministry and for general pastoral and religious leadership responsibilities in congregations and other settings." Association of Theological Schools, "Degree Program Standards," A.1.1.1 accessed May 30, 2017, http://docs.ats.edu/uploads/accrediting/documents/educational-and-degree-program-standards.pdf,

letters, serve to advise and encourage pastors like Timothy and Titus to uprightness in conduct, wisdom in administering the congregation, and the pursuit of correct doctrine. In this sense, Paul's letters to congregations have more in common with a hortatory sermon than a course in a theological institution.

Points of Comparison

Admittedly, Paul's epistles and online theological education have some profound differences, and these differences do not allow for a one-to-one comparison. In a sense, comparing them is like comparing apples and oranges. This does not mean, however, that there are no similarities, no ways in which Paul's epistles and online theological education are comparable. Apples have more in common, for example, with oranges than they do with stones. The following points are offered to help establish a sufficient amount of similarity between Paul's epistles and online theological education to allow for analogical comparison in the use of Paul's epistles to guide online theological education.

Epistle as an educational tool.

Crucial to this comparison is the idea that Paul's epistles were educational—that is, they deliberately attempted to facilitate efforts toward particular goals and outcomes. (Admittedly, neither Paul nor the philosophers would have used the terms "education" or "educational." However, this does not entail that this section is anachronistic. Rather, this section acknowledges that Paul and the philosophers conducted what modern people call education, even though the ancients did not themselves use this term.) To that end, the Greco-Roman letter writing tradition must be considered. In the first-century context, letters were frequently used for educational purposes. For example, philosophical schools, most notably the Stoics and Cynics, readily used the letter in their efforts to instruct students.[7] While this point cannot be estab-

---

emphasis added. Paul's focus on providing instruction to congregations rather than individuals was unique in his day as well. Stanley Kent Stowers, *Letter Writing in Greco-Roman Antiquity* (Philadelphia: Westminster Press, 1986), 42–43.

[7] Stowers, *Letter Writing in Greco-Roman Antiquity*, 36–40; William G. Doty, *Letters in Primitive Christianity* (Philadelphia: Fortress Press, 1973), 6–7.

lished with absolute certainty, evidence indicates that Paul adapted the epistolary conventions of the philosophers toward his particular ends. Paul certainly had contact with the philosophers (Acts 17), and his letters show many similarities to Greco-Roman philosophical letters, similarities that would suggest his use and adaptation of these philosophical letters.[8] In sum, evidence from outside of Paul's epistles and evidence within them suggests that Paul considered his epistles similarly to the philosophers as means of offering instruction.

The content of the epistles also indicates that Paul considered his letters to be means of facilitating learning, means of what moderns now call education. First, some epistles mainly contain doctrinal content—Romans and Galatians are the best examples. Other epistles had exhortation or the teaching of ethics and morals as their aim. And yet, many of Paul's urgings have a theological basis. For example, Paul grounds his instructions concerning the Lord's Supper (1 Cor 11:33–34) upon doctrine (1 Cor 11:23–26).[9] Furthermore, Paul states forthrightly that he intends his epistles to perform theological instruction. For instance, Colossians 1:24–28 demonstrates that Paul considered his epistles to be a means of theological education. Paul indicates that God commissioned him to instruct the Colossians (v. 25).

---

[8] Stowers, *Letter Writing in Greco-Roman Antiquity*, 42; John L. White, *The Form and Function of the Body of the Greek Letter: A Study of the Letter-Body in the Non-Literary Papyri and in Paul the Apostle*, SBL Dissertation Series 2 (Missoula, MT: Published by Scholars Press for the Society of Biblical Literature, 1972), 159; John L. White, *Light from Ancient Letters* (Philadelphia: Fortress Press, 1986), 192; Abraham J. Malherbe, "'Gentle as a Nurse': The Cynic Background to I Thess II," *Novum Testamentum* 12, no. 2 (April 1, 1970): 203–17, doi:10.2307/1560046; Abraham J. Malherbe, *Paul and the Popular Philosophers* (Minneapolis: Fortress Press, 1989).

[9] This characteristic method of Paul, in which he conveys doctrine in response to challenges or questions faced in congregational life, is unique. This focus on congregational issues puts his letters in a different category than the philosophical treatise in epistle form, but the universal doctrinal content he relates to such local concerns precludes his epistles from being merely letters of exhortation. Doty, *Letters in Primitive Christianity*, 25–27, 42. Barnett states that 2 Corinthians 10:3–6 is another example of Paul giving timeless teaching motivated from a "mundane situation." Paul Barnett, *The Second Epistle to the Corinthians* (Grand Rapids: Eerdmans, 1997), 470.

The epistle and online formats.

The epistle format and online formats have other similarities as well. First, both the epistle and online education are designed to allow communication between people who are not physically close. Second, influencing local congregations is a central concern in both formats. As has been discussed, most of Paul's epistles were written to congregations as a whole. Also, the pastoral epistles were written to pastors actively serving congregations. Only one epistle, Philemon, does not seem to have the congregation in view. Likewise, online theological formats are often pursued both by students and theological institutions to allow students to remain in their current congregations.[10] While theological education, especially traditional approaches to theological education, aim at forming individual students, online programs often keep local congregations as a central concern. Much of their appeal lies in the ability of students to continue their studies while continuing to serve a local congregation, and some programs make use of a student's local context as an integral part of the program.

Another similarity between the epistle and online education is the fact that they have both advantages and limitations as means of communication. Some of the ancient writers considered letters to be just as good as face-to-face communication.[11] But Paul takes a soberer view. Robert Funk has convincingly shown that Paul believed the letter to be less effective as a means of communication than face-to-face interaction:

> The letter, the dispatch of an emissary, and Paul's own presence represent the implementation of the apostolic *parousia* and in ascending order of significance. The presence of Paul in person will therefore be the primary medium by which he makes his apostolic authority effective, whether for negative (1 Cor. 4:19) or positive (Phil. 1:24 ff.) reasons. Letter and envoy will be substitutes, less effective perhaps, but sometimes

---

10 See, for example, Concordia Seminary, "Specific Ministry Pastor (SMP)," accessed September 19, 2012, http://www.csl.edu/admissions/academics/altrt/specific-ministry-pastor-smp-pastor/.
11 Stowers, *Letter Writing in Greco-Roman Antiquity*, 36–40; William G. Doty, *Letters in Primitive Christianity* (Philadelphia: Fortress Press, 1973), 6–7.

necessary. The shape of the apostolic *parousia* as a whole should be considered from this perspective.[12]

Despite this sober view, Paul at times acknowledged that the epistle could be a better means of communication than his personal presence in some circumstances.[13] Likewise, even proponents of online education, while arguing for certain advantages of that medium, have noted that such a format has limitations as a means of communication.[14]

Sufficiently Comparable

As is the case for all instances of analogical reasoning, significant differences exist between the two domains under consideration. However, the presence of such differences does not delegitimize the rendering of an analogy between the Pauline epistles and online theological education. While these differences necessitate a certain modesty or cautiousness in rendering judgments regarding online theological education on the basis of Pauline epistolary theory and practice, the similarities between these two domains do allow one to make such modest or cautious judgments. Despite the differences between Pauline epistolary practice and online theological education, they have enough in

---

12 Robert W. Funk, "The Apostolic *Parousia*: Form and Significance," in *Christian History and Interpretation: Studies Presented to John Knox*, ed. John Knox et al. (Cambridge: Cambridge University Press, 1967), 258. Some scholars have disagreed with Funk, stating his paradigm downplays the effectiveness and power vested in Paul's letters. Wall notes that Paul uses the threat of a visit to heighten the authority of a letter, "which supplies an inferior *although effective* substitute for Paul's persona and the edifying charisms he conveys within the faith community." Robert W. Wall, "The Function of the Pastoral Letters within the Pauline Canon of the New Testament: A Canonical Approach," in *The Pauline Canon*, ed. Stanley E. Porter, Pauline Studies, v. 1 (Atlanta: Society of Biblical Literature, 2009), 30. Emphasis added.

13 Christopher Dwight Jackson, "The Phenomenon of Social Presence in the Pauline Epistles and Its Implication for Practices of Online Education" (The Southern Baptist Theological Seminary, 2015), 62.

14 Charlotte N. Gunawardena, "Social Presence Theory and Implications for Interaction and Collaborative Learning in Computer Conferences," *International Journal of Educational Telecommunications* 1, no. 2 (1995): 156. Peter Shea, Chun Sau Li, and Alexandra Pickett, "A Study of Teaching Presence and Student Sense of Learning Community in Fully Online and Web-Enhanced College Courses," *The Internet and Higher Education* 9, no. 3 (2006): 175–90.

common to justify treating them as comparable phenomena. Indeed, they are both means of theological education. They are both done from a physical distance. The local congregation is a significant focus in both formats. Both have certain advantages and disadvantages as a means of communication.

Paul and Presence

Having established that it is permissible to make analogical comparisons between the Pauline epistles and online theological education, the following will examine how Paul used the epistle in conducting his ministry in order to make such comparisons.

Apostolic Parousia

Funk's seminal article, "The Apostolic *Parousia*: Form and Significance," provides important insight into Paul's epistles and their purpose.[15] Funk studied a discrete section present in many Pauline epistles: the travelogue.[16] His studies of travelogues led him to discover this:

> Paul regarded his apostolic presence to his congregations under three different but related aspects at once: the aspect of the letter, the apostolic emissary, and his own personal presence. All of these are media by which Paul makes his apostolic authority effective in the churches.[17]

Funk's argument progresses by analyzing Paul's travelogue/*parousia* passages, discussing the paradigm of the visit/emissary/letter discovered through this analysis, and finally applying this implication to current issues in Pauline epistolography. What matters to this chapter most is the paradigm that Funk discovered:

---

15 Funk, "Apostolic *Parousia*." *Parousia* is a transliteration of a Greek word that means, roughly, "presence."
16 Ibid., 249. For a larger discussion of the travelogue as a unit, see Robert Walter Funk, "The Letter: Form and Style," in *Language, Hermeneutic, and Word of God: The Problem of Language in the New Testament and Contemporary Theology* (New York: Harper & Row, 1966), 250–74.
17 Funk, "Apostolic *Parousia*," 249.

The letter, the dispatch of an emissary, and Paul's personal presence represent the implementation of the apostolic *parousia* and in ascending order of significance. The presence of Paul in person will therefore be the primary medium by which he makes his apostolic authority effective. . . . Letter and envoy will be substitutes, less effective perhaps, but sometimes necessary.[18]

Funk indicates that this priority is due to Paul's understanding about his own personal presence as well as his preference for the oral word. Paul preferred to demonstrate his apostolic authority in person because he "thought of his presence as the bearer of charismatic, one might even say, eschatological power."[19] If unable to visit, Paul tended to consider the emissary a more effective means of carrying out his ministry than the letter. The emissary "substitutes for the apostle himself, while the letter is at best written authority for what the emissary has to say. Since Paul gives precedence to the oral word, the written word will not function as a primary medium of his apostleship."[20] Though Paul considers the letter to be the least effective means of exercising his apostolic *parousia*, it is nevertheless a "surrogate for his presence, with which . . . the letter is entirely congruent."[21]

Funk's explanation of the Pauline paradigm for his apostolic *parousia*, while accurate, widely cited, and helpful, is however prone to abuse. Some interpret Funk to mean that Paul held disparaging thoughts concerning his letters. For example, Doty states, "It may well be that Paul considered a letter to be a fairly poor substitute for his personal presence and the spoken word . . . ," and cites Funk for this assertion.[22] Diekema and Caddell cite Funk in questioning the use of Paul's epistles as a justification for online theological education.[23]

However, just because Paul considered his letters to be the least effective means of influencing his congregations does not mean that

18 Ibid., 258.
19 Ibid., 265.
20 Ibid., 260.
21 Ibid., 266.
22 Doty, *Letters in Primitive Christianity*, v.
23 D. P. Caddell and D. A. Diekema, "Response: The Chimera of Virtual Place: False Dichotomies Never Apply," *Christian Scholar's Review* 32, no. 1 (2002): 27–29. "Response," 27–29, gives several objections to the use of Paul.

he held disparaging thoughts regarding them. Paul was certainly aware of the limitations of the letter, and sometimes these limitations even caused him anxiety. Yet, Paul at times indicates that the letter was even more effective than a visit would have been. On one occasion, he even appeals to a letter in order to build confidence in his personal presence. Paul had a sober but high view of the letter, not a disparaging one, as the next section will demonstrate.

Points Concerning Pauline Epistolary Theory and Practice

This section will summarize Paul's views concerning the use of epistles. While the following seven points are not a comprehensive summary of Paul's beliefs about his letters, they do provide a basis of comparison with online theological education.[24]

1. Paul believed that in most circumstances he could dispatch his apostolic mission, including instruction in Christian doctrine and morality, most effectively in person. Paul generally preferred carrying out his apostolic mission in person. Letters and envoys or emissaries are useful, but they could not accomplish all that Paul could in a visit (Rom 1:8–10). Paul shows this conviction in Romans, where he expresses a continued desire to visit the church despite the fact that he had already written a letter (Rom 1:9, 11; 15:14–33).[25] Paul believed that his personal presence not only afforded the opportunity for preaching (Rom 1:15) but also for providing an example of proper Christian living, especially for new believers (1 Cor 4:16–17).[26] Paul also feared that his epistles may not fully convey his love and concern for the churches

---

[24] These seven points are based on Paul's own statements regarding his epistles. While Funk's *parousia* passages provide the backbone of these statements, other statements not included in Funk's list are cited. These were not included in Funk's article because they are not part of a travelogue. For more thorough discussions of each of the passages cited, see Jackson, "The Phenomenon of Social Presence in the Pauline Epistles and Its Implication for Practices of Online Education," chap. 3.

[25] Joseph A. Fitzmyer, *Romans: A New Translation with Introduction and Commentary* (New York: Doubleday, 1993), 248.

[26] Ibid.; Thomas R. Schreiner, *Romans*, Baker Exegetical Commentary on the New Testament 6 (Grand Rapids: Baker, 1998), 58; Willis Peter De Boer, "The Imitation of Paul: An Exegetical Study" (Vrije Universiteit, Amsterdam, 1962), 213–14; C. K. Barrett, *The First Epistle to the Corinthians*, Black's New Testament Commentary (Peabody, MA: Hendrickson, 1993), 116.

(Gal 4:12–20).[27] Paul fears that it may be easier for the members of his churches to stray from Christian morality when he is away (Phil 1:27).[28] Finally, Paul used personal visits as a means of vesting his letters with authority (Phil 2:24; Phlm 21–22).[29]

2. Paul believed that his presence could be mediated by means of the epistle. As other ancient writers, Paul believed that a letter could bear the authority of an author.[30] Paul discharges "his apostolic missionary obligation" of preaching the gospel to the Romans by means of composing his epistle (Rom 1:8–15).[31] Also, by means of the epistle, Paul exercises an authoritative spiritual presence by which he sits in judgment among the Corinthians (1 Cor 5:3–5).[32] The Paul who is present is the same Paul of his letters (2 Cor 10:11).[33] He uses the letter to reinforce and drive home the message he has delivered in person, and he strives through his language to create the impression that he is actually among the hearers of his epistle (1 Thess 3:4).[34] At times, Paul expresses confidence that his letters will result in the obedience of his hearers (Phlm 21–22). Even though Paul gave the letter the least

---

27 F. F. Bruce, *The Epistle to the Galatians: A Commentary on the Greek Text* (Grand Rapids: Eerdmans, 1982), 213.
28 G. Walter Hansen, *The Letter to the Philippians* (Grand Rapids; Nottingham, England: Eerdmans; Apollos, 2009), 95; Moisés Silva, *Philippians* (Grand Rapids: Baker Academic, 2005), 81.
29 Hansen, *The Letter to the Philippians*, 192, 198; Peter Thomas O'Brien, *Colossians, Philemon* (Waco, TX: Word, 1982), 36.
30 See "Persona Transmitted through the Epistle," in Jackson, "The Phenomenon of Social Presence in the Pauline Epistles and Its Implication for Practices of Online Education," chap. 2.
31 Fitzmyer, *Romans*, 248.
32 C. K. Barrett, *The First Epistle to the Corinthians*, 123–24; Joseph A. Fitzmyer, *First Corinthians: A New Translation with Introduction and Commentary*, Anchor Bible, vol. 32 (New Haven: Yale University Press, 2008), 236; Gordon D. Fee, *The First Epistle to the Corinthians*, New International Commentary on the New Testament (Grand Rapids: Eerdmans, 1987), 255; David E. Garland, *1 Corinthians*, Baker Exegetical Commentary on the New Testament (Grand Rapids: Baker, 2003), 164–65; Anthony C. Thiselton, *The First Epistle to the Corinthians: A Commentary on the Greek Text*, New International Greek Testament Commentary (Grand Rapids: Eerdmans, 2000), 391.
33 Barnett, *The Second Epistle to the Corinthians*, 478.
34 Ben Witherington, *1 and 2 Thessalonians: A Socio-Rhetorical Commentary* (Grand Rapids: Eerdmans, 2006), 94; Jane M. F. Heath, "Absent Presences of Paul and Christ: *Enargeia* in 1 Thessalonians 1–3," *Journal for the Study of the New Testament* 32, no. 1 (2009): 5.

priority out of the three means of exercising his apostolic *parousia*, he yet considered his letters to be an effective means.[35]

3. Paul believed that in some circumstances his personal presence would be less effective than an emissary or a letter. In one circumstance, Paul believed that a personal visit would cause unnecessary pain to both him and the Corinthians, and this belief led him to send the "Severe Letter" (2 Cor 2:3–4).[36] In another circumstance, Paul believed that sending an emissary would encourage the Corinthians to give freely; whereas, if Paul were to be present, the collection would be an exaction (2 Cor 9:5).[37] As Funk argues, the letter and the emissary in these circumstances prepare the way for a personal visit, and thus they do not represent a reordering of the priority of Paul's apostolic *parousia*. Still, the fact remains that a visit in these circumstances would have been counterproductive to Paul's greater apostolic mission.[38]

4. Paul's personal presence and epistolary presence mutually reinforced each other. At times Paul's epistles prepared the way for a future apostolic visit (2 Cor 2:3–4).[39] At other times, the epistle reinforced what Paul had taught in his visits (1 Thess 3:4).[40] And always, the promise of a visit heightened the authority of his letters (Phil 2:24; Phlm 21–22).[41] In turn, the strength of his letters lent credibility to his ministry in person (2 Cor 10:11). Yes, Paul favored the personal visit as generally the most effective means of exercising his apostolic *parousia*. But, it does not follow that the legitimacy of his letters flowed only from his visits. Visits, or promises of visits, strengthened the effectiveness of his letters. However, his letters carried a legitimacy independent of the visit, so that his letter could also strengthen the effectiveness of his visits.

---

35   Funk, "Apostolic *Parousia*," 258; Wall, "The Function of the Pastoral Letters Within the Pauline Canon of the New Testament: A Canonical Approach," 30.
36   Barrett, *The Second Epistle to the Corinthians*, 87; Ernest Best, *Second Corinthians*, Interpretation, a Bible Commentary for Teaching and Preaching (Atlanta: J. Knox Press, 1987), 21; Barnett, *The Second Epistle to the Corinthians*, 119; Furnish, *II Corinthians*, 159.
37   Murray J. Harris, *The Second Epistle to the Corinthians: A Commentary on the Greek Text* (Grand Rapids; Milton Keynes, UK: Eerdmans; Paternoster Press, 2005), 629; Barnett, *The Second Epistle to the Corinthians*, 434–35.
38   Funk, "Apostolic *Parousia*," 259, note 1.
39   Ibid.
40   Witherington, *1 and 2 Thessalonians*, 94.
41   Hansen, *The Letter to the Philippians*, 192, 198; O'Brien, *Colossians, Philemon*, 36.

5. Paul used the epistle as part of a cohesive strategy for fulfilling his apostolic mission. Paul was aware of the strengths and weaknesses of the various means of carrying out his apostolic mission. He understood that some circumstances called for a personal visit while others demanded a letter. At times, he recognized that a visit could be counterproductive and that a letter served his purposes better. On other occasions, his letters and his visits mutually reinforced each other. Thus, one cannot legitimately view Paul's letters as merely supplemental to his visits.[42] Rather, Paul deliberately used the letter as an integral part of a cohesive strategy. His ministry would have been less effective had he not used the letter.

6. Paul was cautiously optimistic that his disposition could be perceived by his letter's audience. Paul takes pains to disclose intimate details of the heart in his letters (Rom 1:10; 1 Thess 2:17–18).[43] That he included such inner thoughts indicates that Paul believed they could be appreciated by the audience. However, some passages indicate that Paul feared that his disposition of love and concern would not carry through the text of his letter (Gal 4:20).[44] Paul was therefore not entirely comfortable in the letter's ability to convey his disposition.

7. Paul wanted to create the sense that he was personally present by means of the epistle. Ancient official letters held a place of authority and conveyed the sense that the authority figure was actually present.[45] Because the ancients considered letters to be one half of a conversation, they emphasized that the writers of letters should strive to imitate conversational speech and reflect the writer's personality.[46] Paul utilized this epistolary convention. He states that by means of

---

42   Contrary to House, "Hewing to Scripture's Pattern: A Plea for Personal Theological Education," 4.
43   Adolf Deissmann, *Light from the Ancient East: The New Testament Illustrated by Recently Discovered Texts of the Graeco-Roman World*, trans. Lionel Richard Mortimer Strachan, 4th ed. (New York: George H. Doran, 1927), 240–41; Paul Schubert, "Form and Function of the Pauline Letters," *The Journal of Religion* 19, no. 4 (October 1, 1939): 376; Witherington, *1 and 2 Thessalonians*, 100; Abraham J. Malherbe, *Paul and the Popular Philosophers* (Minneapolis: Fortress Press, 1989), 75.
44   Bruce, *The Epistle to the Galatians*, 213.
45   Doty, *Letters in Primitive Christianity*, 6.
46   Abraham J. Malherbe, *Ancient Epistolary Theorists* (Atlanta: Scholars Press, 1988), 12; White, *Light from Ancient Letters*, 191.

the epistle he is sitting in a place of authority among the Corinthians (1 Cor 5:3–5).[47] He attempts to conjure a sense among the Thessalonians that he is personally among them (1 Thess 3:4).[48]

Conclusion

When making comparisons to online theological education, most discussions of Paul's epistles have focused on the externals: the fact that he wrote them, how they were delivered, what audiences received them, and so on. These are important points that must be considered. However, this chapter has examined not just Paul's epistolary practice but also his theory. This examination has been conducted only after establishing that Paul's epistolary practice and theory can be brought to bear on the theory and practice of online education via analogical reasoning. While demonstrating that Paul gave a priority to conducting his apostolic ministry by means of his physical presence, this chapter has also shown that Paul believed that his epistles were a means of being personally present. In addition, this chapter has shown that Paul believed that his epistles had authority and legitimacy independent of his personal visits. These points offer strong guidance for the theory and practice of online theological education by means of analogy, and such guidance will be provided in the next chapter's applications and recommendations.

---

47   Barrett, *The First Epistle to the Corinthians*, 123–24; Fitzmyer, *First Corinthians*, 236; Fee, *The First Epistle to the Corinthians*, 255; Garland, *1 Corinthians*, 164–65; Thiselton, *The First Epistle to the Corinthians*, 391.
48   Heath, "Absent Presences of Paul and Christ," 5.

Opportunities for Application

Discover

> Analyze Paul's letters, looking for examples of the possibility of "absent presence."

Decide

> Determine, on the basis of Paul's epistolary practices, strengths and weaknesses of theological education in the absence of personal presence.

Do

> Evaluate syllabi for online courses in your institution, looking for ways in which professors are effectively compensating for the absence of personal presence.

CHAPTER 3

Social Presence and Theological Education

The previous chapter examined the past in a very specific way. It examined the views of a particular individual from ancient times. That examination is important and vital; however, the purpose of this book is to guide individuals and institutions that are concerned about a present-day issue: online theological education. This chapter will bridge the gap from the historical and particular to the contemporary and general by making recommendations for online theological education on the basis of Pauline epistolary theory and practice.

The Concept of Social Presence

In order to apply Pauline epistolary theory and practice to contemporary practices of online theological education, it is necessary to translate, or shift, the manner of speaking to reflect the differences between online media and the Pauline epistles. The language developed by contemporary social presence theory offers a fruitful vocabulary to do this work of translation insofar as it offers a broader way of speaking about the sense of personal presence through media in a way that includes, but is not limited to, the letter.

The previous chapter contended that Paul believed his letters could make his persona and ethos evident to his audiences.[1] In recent decades, social scientists have studied the sense of interacting with a real person through media under the term "social presence," first coined by Short, Williams, and Christie.[2] They use this term to describe the capacity for any particular communication medium to communicate the ethos of individuals.[3] In other words, they believe that certain media were better at facilitating an individual's communication of his or her personality than others. Face-to-face communication would have greater social presence than communication over the telephone, which does not allow for facial expressions or other such bodily cues.[4] Yet, telephone communication would have greater social presence than letter writing. In order to flesh out their theory, Short, Williams, and Christie drew upon the idea of intimacy as discussed by Argyle and Dean and the idea of immediacy as discussed by Wiener and Mehrabian.[5] Again, Short, Williams, and Christie focused on what was perceived to be objective qualities of various communication media. Some media, for example, are better at conveying a sense of intimacy, the feelings of closeness that one has with regard to the other with whom one is speaking. Additionally, the type of medium is a way of conveying immediacy, the cues of the psychological or emotional closeness or distance given by a communicator. Two things should be noted about this discussion of Short, Williams, and Christie. First, they discussed intimacy and immediacy in terms of the communication medium itself: the use of a particular medium conveys a particular sense of intimacy or immediacy. Second, they discussed intimacy

---

1   The idea that the letters of Paul could make his persona and ethos present to his audiences is contrary to Diekema and Caddell's thought that Paul's letters only conveyed a "'sense' of his presence." Diekema and Caddell, "Response," 29. Further reflection on how Paul's letters mediated his presence in part necessitates the appeal to social presence theory.
2   John Short, Ederyn Williams, and Bruce Christie, "Theoretical Approaches to Differences between Media," in *The Social Psychology of Telecommunications* (London: Wiley, 1976).
3   Ibid., 65.
4   Ibid., 75–76.
5   Ibid., 72–73; Morton Wiener and Albert Mehrabian, *Language Within Language: Immediacy, A Channel in Verbal Communication* (New York: Appleton-Century-Crofts, 1968); Michael Argyle and Janet Dean, "Eye Contact, Distance, and Affiliation," *Sociometry* 28, no. 3 (1965): 289–304.

and immediacy as related concepts to social presence, but they did not necessarily consider them to be constitutive elements of social presence.[6]

The next step in social presence theory came from Rafaeli.[7] Rafaeli somewhat modified the idea of social presence held by Short, Williams, and Christie to make it more subjective. Social presence, for Rafaeli, was the sense in which participants engaged in communication felt like they were engaged with a real person, based upon their perceptions of intimacy and immediacy with the other communicator. It should be noted that Rafaeli questioned the utility of social presence as a helpful idea in the analysis of communication.[8] However, Rafaeli expanded discussions of social presence by discussing it in more subjective terms, and by introducing the idea that media may have different capacities for facilitating social presence, capacities that can be utilized to a greater or lesser extent by participants in communication. He accomplished this expansion of the discussion of social presence in an indirect way. As previously mentioned, Rafaeli questioned the idea of social presence, and his explorations had more to do with "interactivity," what he described as the "degree to which . . . exchanges referred to even earlier transmissions."[9] However, Rafaeli influenced discussions of social presence, despite his reluctance to embrace the idea, through his insight concerning interactivity: certain media have more or less capability of facilitating interactivity, but that capability may also be utilized by communicators to a greater or lesser extent.[10]

The idea that different communication media have different capacities for what Rafaeli termed "interactivity," but that those utilizing these media could use them to greater or lesser effect, was taken up later by Walther.[11] Walther was among the first to notice that theories

---

6   Short, Williams, and Christie, "Theoretical Approaches to Differences," 72.
7   S. Rafaeli, "Interactivity: From New Media to Communication," in *Advancing Communication Science: Merging Mass and Interpersonal Processes*, ed. Robert Hawkins, John M. Wiemann, and Suzanne Pingree (Newbury Park, CA: Sage, 1988), 110–34; idem, "Interaction with Media: Parasocial Interaction and Real Interaction," in *Information and Behavior*, ed. Brent D. Ruben and Leah A. Lievrouw (New Brunswick, NJ: Transaction, 1990), 3:125–81.
8   Ibid., 117.
9   Ibid., 111.
10 Ibid.
11 Joseph B. Walther, "Interpersonal Effects in Computer-Mediated Interaction: A Relational Perspective," *Communication Research* 19, no. 1 (1992): 52–90.

regarding the possibility of building relationships and community through computer-mediated conferencing did not match the results of early studies, which found that participants in computer-mediated conferencing did feel that it was possible to build true relationships and community online.[12] However, he did have a few caveats. Specifically, he believed that computer-mediated formats have what is now called "low social bandwidth," although he did not use this term. In other words, his impression was that it took longer to create relationships and community through online formats. However, despite this limitation he believed that those who apply themselves in the online format could attain real relationships on a par with relationships that were fostered face-to-face.[13] Walther's work, more than anything, was a call for a research agenda. Specifically, he noted that much more work needed to be done to explore the impressions of those engaged in computer-mediated formats as to the intimacy and immediacy they felt with others engaged in conversation with them.[14]

That research agenda has been taken up by many; however, Gunawardena has been the foremost in conducting this research.[15]

---

12   Ibid., 52–54.
13   Ibid., 80.
14   Ibid., 81–82.
15   Charlotte N. Gunawardena, "Social Presence Theory and Implications for Interaction and Collaborative Learning in Computer Conferences," *International Journal of Educational Telecommunications* 1, no. 2 (1995): 137–66; Charlotte N. Gunawardena and Frank J. Zittle, "Social Presence as Predictor of Satisfaction within a Computer-Mediated Conferencing Environment," *The American Journal of Distance Education* 11, no. 3 (1997): 101–17; Kayleigh Carabajal, Deborah LaPointe, and Charlotte N. Gunawardena, "Group Development in Online Learning Communities," in *Handbook of Distance Education*, ed. Michael G. Moore and William G. Anderson (Mahwah, NJ: Erlbaum, 2003): 217–34; Charlotte N. Gunawardena et al., "A Theoretical Framework for Building Online Communities of Practice with Social Networking Tools," *Educational Media International* 46, no. 1 (2009): 3–16; Charlotte N. Gunawardena, C. A. Lowe, and T. Anderson, "Analysis of a Global Online Debate and the Development of an Interaction Analysis Model for Examining Social Construction of Knowledge in Computer Conference," *Journal of Educational Computing Research* 17, no. 4 (1997): 397–431; Charlotte N. Gunawardena et al., "A Cross-Cultural Study of Group Process and Development in Online Conferences," *Distance Education* 22, no. 1 (2001): 85–121; Daniel C. A. Hillman, Deborah J. Willis, and Charlotte N. Gunawardena, "Learner-Interface Interaction in Distance Education: An

Gunawardena's work supports this book in three ways. First, she has conducted studies that confirm Walther's theory. Her research notes that it is more difficult to build relationships and therefore community within computer-mediated conferencing formats, but she also observed that participants within these formats, recognizing this difficulty, take special effort to project their persona in order to facilitate interpersonal relationships.[16] In other words, social presence is more difficult to facilitate in online formats than face-to-face, but by utilizing practices that lead to immediacy and intimacy, social presence can happen. Second, Gunawardena draws upon a substantial research base with regard to the importance of instructors displaying behaviors associated with immediacy.[17] The weight of these studies is that the displaying of immediacy behaviors by a teacher is correlated to student success, whether in face-to-face or online formats, confirming the theory that social bandwidth can be utilized to a greater or lesser extent. Third, Gunawardena's work indicates that students who have a heightened sense of the social presence with their instructors and peers tend to report greater satisfaction with their online coursework.[18]

A few authors have applied the idea of social presence to online education, including Mark R. Maddix, James Riley Estep, and Mary

Extension of Contemporary Models and Strategies for Practitioners," *American Journal of Distance Education* 8, no. 2 (1994): 30–42; Deborah K. LaPointe and Charlotte N. Gunawardena, "Developing, Testing and Refining of a Model to Understand the Relationship between Peer Interaction and Learning Outcomes in Computer-Mediated Conferencing," *Distance Education* 25, no. 1 (2004): 83–106; M. S. McIsaac and Charlotte N. Gunawardena, "Distance Education," in *Handbook of Research for Educational Communications and Technology*, ed. David H. Jonassen (New York: Mac, 1996), 403–37.

16   Gunawardena, "Social Presence Theory," 163–65.
17   Ibid., 152–53; Derek H. Kelley and Joan Gorham, "Effects of Immediacy on Recall of Information," *Communication Education* 37, no. 3 (July 1988): 198–207; Diane M. Christophel, "The Relationships among Teacher Immediacy Behaviors, Student Motivation, and Learning," *Communication Education* 39, no. 4 (1990): 323–40; P. Kearney, T. Plax, and N. Wendt-Wasco, "Teacher Immediacy for Affective Learning in Divergent College Classes," *Communication Quarterly* 3, no. 1 (1985): 61–74; Joan Gorham, "The Relationship between Verbal Teacher Immediacy Behaviors and Student Learning," *Communication Education* 37, no. 1 (1988): 40–54.
18   Gunawardena and Zittle, "Social Presence as Predictor," 23.

Hinkle Shore.[19] Their work tends to emphasize the importance of attending to social presence in order to build a sense of immediacy between students and their instructors and in order to build community in online learning formats. While these observations are certainly valid and helpful, no connection has been made between the idea of social presence and the appropriateness of online learning formats in theological education. This chapter, on the other hand, draws lines of comparison between the apparent Pauline sense of the possibility of conveying presence through his epistles, contemporary notions of social presence, and the ideals of theological education, in order to show that indeed there is biblical precedent for thinking that goals such as spiritual and character formation, and even the fostering of community, can in fact happen through online formats.

> **Social Presence**
>
> The degree to which individuals feel that they are interacting with a real person.

Social Presence in Paul's Letters

The following four points lay out the case that social presence theory can legitimately be used to discuss Paul's views concerning his presence via the epistle.

1. The language of social presence theory can legitimately be used to describe means by which Paul exercised personal presence through his epistles. No anachronism is involved in using social presence theory to analyze the Pauline epistles. It is not being claimed, for example, that Paul had a sense of contemporary social presence theory. Rather, this chapter uses the language of social presence theory to describe Paul's belief that his hearers could have a greater or lesser sense of interacting with a real person in his letters as well as Paul's means by which he sought to foster that sense.

That Paul believed he could be personally present by means of his letters, albeit in a less effective way than in a personal visit, has already

---

19 Mark A. Maddix, "Developing Online Learning Communities," in *Best Practices of Online Education*, ed. Mark Maddix, James Estep, and Mary Lowe (Information Age Publishing, 2012), 31–40; James Riley Estep, "Social Presence in Online Learning," in *Best Practices of Online Education*, 41–54; Mary Hinkle Shore, "Establishing Social Presence in Online Courses: Why and How," *Theological Education* 42, no. 2 (2007): 91–100.

been explored in the previous chapter. Paul's attempted arousal of a strong sense of his presence can be understood as one of many approaches to heightening intimacy within his letters. This point does not claim that Paul consciously adhered to some nascent form of contemporary social presence theory. Such a claim would clearly be anachronistic. Rather, this chapter suggests that social presence theory, as a descriptive paradigm to explain how individuals come to have a sense that one is interacting with a real person, is useful when it comes to describing Paul's beliefs concerning his ability to be personally present among those who received his letters.

2. Paul believed that recipients of letters could have a greater or lesser sense of interacting with a real person, a greater or lesser sense of social presence. Ancient epistolary theorists believed that letters were one half of a dialogue and that the skilled author of letters would strive to make his personality shine through the text.[20] Ancient theorists desired that reading a letter would give the impression of interacting with its sender in person:

> Seneca stated that he wanted his letters to be just like the conversation he would speak if he were actually sitting or walking in one's company, and that he wanted nothing strange or artificial in his letters. Likening the letter to actual conversation, Julius Victor advised one to use expressions which recognize the recipient's presence, such as "you too?" And "just as you say!" And "I see you smile."[21]

Paul not only adopted this epistolary convention of self-disclosure, but he also took it to extremes not normally seen among the ancients.[22] Paul was aware of the desirability for recipients of letters to have the impression of interacting with the sender in person and therefore took great pain to ensure that his readers gained that impression.[23] Though Paul would not have been aware of this terminology, in his letters he

---

20 Malherbe, *Ancient Epistolary Theorists*, 12; White, *Light from Ancient Letters*, 191.
21 White, *Light from Ancient Letters*, 191.
22 Deissmann, *Light from the Ancient East*, 240–41; Schubert, "Form and Function of the Pauline Letters," 376; William G. Doty, "Classification of Epistolary Literature," *Catholic Biblical Quarterly* 31, no. 2 (April 1, 1969): 2.
23 Heath, "Absent Presences of Paul and Christ," 5.

fostered social presence, the impression that one is interacting with a real person.

3. Paul sought to increase social presence by fostering intimacy, feelings of closeness to him by his audience. Paul took to extremes the ideal of self-disclosure recommended by ancient epistolary theorists.[24] Such radical self-disclosure can be seen, for example, in 1 Thessalonians 2:17, where "one . . . cannot but be touched by the deep pathos of the text and the profound love and concern exuding from Paul."[25] This radical self-disclosure, a deliberate choice on Paul's part, was aimed in part to arouse feelings of closeness toward him in his readers. In other words, Paul attempted to foster intimacy in his hearers.[26]

4. Paul sought to increase social presence by fostering immediacy, cues of accessibility to his audience. Paul intended to highlight his authority over his audiences. Paul utilized the official letter type as a means of exercising authority among his congregations.[27] At the same time, Paul used verbal cues to express accessibility to his hearers. He adopts tones of equality with his readers, utilizing such terms as "brothers" (1 Thess 2:17) and indicating that a visit would give mutual benefit (Rom 1:11–12). Mixing such authoritative and egalitarian tones was a Pauline innovation, indicating that a deliberate choice was made and that Paul was not merely following convention.[28] Therefore, Paul deliberately sought to foster immediacy, cues of accessibility toward his audiences.[29]

---

24 Deissmann, *Light from the Ancient East*, 240–41; Schubert, "Form and Function of the Pauline Letters," 376; Doty, "Classification of Epistolary Literature," 2.
25 Witherington, *1 and 2 Thessalonians*, 100.
26 Michael Argyle and Janet Dean, "Eye Contact, Distance, and Affiliation," *Sociometry* 28, no. 3 (1965): 293.
27 Doty, *Letters in Primitive Christianity*, 6; White, *Light from Ancient Letters*, 218.
28 White, *Light from Ancient Letters*, 219; Stowers, *Letter Writing in Greco-Roman Antiquity*, 27–31.
29 Morton Wiener and Albert Mehrabian, *Language within Language: Immediacy, a Channel in Verbal Communication* (New York: Appleton-Century-Crofts, 1968), 289–304.

Implications

This section explores the implications, the applications and recommendations for practice, that derive from a proper understanding of Paul's epistolary theory and practice.

Applications for Today

1. Pauline epistolary theory and practice suggest that traditional, face-to-face formats should hold a primary place in theological education. This application may be surprising in a chapter seeking to provide justification and guidance for theological programs utilizing online formats. However, this conclusion cannot be avoided given the evidence. To put it succinctly, if perhaps a bit too colloquially, Paul generally esteemed the pulpit over the postal system.

Giving priority to traditional, face-to-face formats does not preclude the use of online formats in theological education, just as the primacy of visitation in Paul's apostolic ministry did not preclude the use of the epistle.[30] Neither does this primacy of traditional educational formats preclude the formation of completely online courses of study or even completely online institutions like Rockbridge Seminary.

Instead, I argue for sober judgment about the utilization of either face-to-face formats or online formats. Proponents of online theological education are justified in their advocacy, but they should take seriously the concerns expressed by many over the use of online formats in theological education.[31] This section strongly critiques the positions of House, Diekema, and Caddell, but they are correct in their concern that certain opportunities for formation are lost in online

---

30 Many other descriptions for the place of face-to-face formats were considered. For example, "preferred" was considered but ultimately rejected since it conveyed a sense that the use of online formats may be less than ideal for a specific student, school, or program. "Primary," and related words like "primacy" and "priority," was chosen as this is the same term used by Funk to describe the place of the visit in Paul's ministry. However, the use of the term "primary" should not be construed to mean that theological education must be pursued mostly in face-to-face formats.

31 Steve Delamarter, "Theological Educators and Their Concerns about Technology," *Teaching Theology & Religion* 8, no. 3 (2005): 135–38, doi:10.1111/j.1467-9647.2005.00237.x.

formats—opportunities like shared meals, prayers, and worship.[32] Theological institutions, accrediting agencies, and potential students should attend to this application when making decisions about the place of online formats in theological education.

2. Pauline epistolary theory and practice suggest that online formats may be legitimately used for theological education. While Paul gave priority to his visits in exercising his apostolic *parousia*, he believed that his letters carried legitimate authority in themselves. He may have generally considered his letters to be less effective than visits, but at times he found them necessary.[33] Like many contemporary theological faculty members, Paul believed in the importance of personally relating to his congregations; however, Paul believed that his personal presence could be mediated by means of the epistle.[34] Likewise, Paul believed that in some circumstances the epistle was a better means of exercising his apostolic authority than a visit. Therefore, Paul utilized the epistle as part of a cohesive strategy in which the epistle and the apostolic visit mutually reinforced each other.

Paul's belief that the letter could legitimately be used should be instructive to detractors of utilizing online formats in theological education. Indeed, this aspect of Paul's epistolary theory would indicate that the use of media such as online formats in theological education is legitimate.

Moreover, Pauline epistolary theory would suggest that the utilization of online formats, even completely online formats, is legitimate independently from their relationship to face-to-face formats. Paul held that his letters carried legitimacy and authority in themselves, independent of an apostolic visit. His letters were not merely supplemental to his visits but were rather an integral part of his greater, cohesive apostolic mission. The legitimacy of Paul's letters, a legitimacy independent of an apostolic visit, would suggest that online theological

---

32 Paul R. House, "Hewing to Scripture's Pattern: A Plea for Personal Theological Education," 2, 6; Diekema and Caddell, "The Significance of Place: Sociological Reflections on Distance Learning and Christian Higher Education," 169–84; Caddell and Diekema, "Response: The Chimera of Virtual Place: False Dichotomies Never Apply," 19–30.
33 Funk, "Apostolic *Parousia*," 258.
34 Delamarter, "Theological Educators," 135–38.

education can legitimately be utilized independent of any relationship to traditional, face-to-face educational formats.[35]

3. The utilization of online formats in theological education is legitimate in part on account of social presence, the sense of interacting with a real person through media. Paul utilized the epistle, over against the philosophical treatise or the play, on account of the epistle's capacity to imitate dialogue as if the writer and reader were physically present and conversing. Paul believed that his presence could be mediated by means of the epistle. Many of Delamarter's respondents were concerned that some of the more "personal" aspects of the theological educational endeavor would be lost online, aspects such as spontaneity, the exhilaration of conversational banter, and the ability to conduct mentoring, character development, and spiritual formation on account of the ease of adopting fake online personae.[36] Paul's epistolary theory and practice would indicate that he, too, sensed the importance of authentic and personal relationships in the task of instructing in Christian doctrine and morality. That Paul yet utilized the letter indicates his confidence that his hearers could have the sense that through the letter they were interacting with the real Paul. He was cautiously optimistic that his disposition when writing could be perceived by a letter's audience, and he strove to give the sense in his epistles that he himself was among them by fostering intimacy and the giving of immediacy cues. Paul believed that it was possible to foster the personal element of theological education within the epistle. Likewise, social presence theory indicates that it is possible to foster authentic personal relationships through online media.

It must be conceded that it is possible to adopt fake persona online. However, it is also possible to adopt fake persona in face-to-face formats. Hypocrisy did not begin with the advent of the Internet. The ability to adopt fake persona online is not a valid reason to discredit online theological education any more than it is a valid reason to discredit face-to-face theological education.

---

35 Contrary to House, who, based on his conviction that the apostolic writings were merely supplemental to the face-to-face ministry of the apostles, recommends that online formats only be used as a bridge to traditional, face-to-face education. House, "Hewing to Scripture's Pattern," 2, 6.

36 Delamarter, "Theological Educators," 135–38.

4. Pauline epistolary theory and practice suggest that online formats may offer opportunities not available in face-to-face, traditional formats. Face-to-face formats are not always the most effective means of delivering theological education. Despite the priority Paul gave to the apostolic visit, he held that the dispatch of an emissary or the sending of a letter could at times be more beneficial to his overall apostolic mission. In like manner, students and theological institutions may find that in some circumstances online formats may better serve their overall mission than face-to-face formats. The Pauline example would indicate that the use of online formats in such circumstances is not only permissible but also recommended. For example, a common use of online formats is certificate programs for laypeople engaged in church work; these are set up in order to give greater theological and biblical understanding.[37] Such a program fills a need that would likely not be met by traditional, face-to-face formats. Additionally, theological institutions may conceivably find certain kinds of conversations lend themselves better to online bulletin boards rather than classroom discussions. For example, the online discussion board may allow for more thoughtful interaction on systematic theology over and against a face-to-face discussion.

5. Theological institutions and faculty should strive to foster social presence in all academic settings, whether online or face-to-face. Social presence is not limited to face-to-face encounters. Paul was optimistic about the ability of the epistle to foster intimacy between him and his readers, but it was a cautious optimism. At times, Paul feared that his disposition of love and concern would not carry through the text of his letter (Gal 4:20).[38] Likewise, social presence is more difficult to build within online formats.[39] The Pauline example would

---

[37] Calvin Theological Seminary, "Certificate Programs," accessed August 27, 2014, http://calvinseminary.edu/academics/certificate-programs/; Covenant Theological Seminary, "Graduate Certificate," accessed August 27, 2014, http://www.covenantseminary.edu/academics/degrees/gc/; Gordon Conwell, "Online Certificate in Christian Studies," accessed August 27, 2014, http://www.gordonconwell.edu/online/Online-Certificate-Christian-Studies.cfm.

[38] F. F. Bruce, *The Epistle to the Galatians: A Commentary on the Greek Text*, New International Greek Testament Commentary (Grand Rapids: Eerdmans, 1982), 213.

[39] Charlotte N. Gunawardena, "Social Presence Theory and Implications for Interaction and Collaborative Learning in Computer Conferences," *International Journal of Educational Telecommunications* 1, no. 2 (1995): 163–65.

indicate, therefore, that the fostering of social presence should be of special concern to students and faculty engaged in online learning.

Theoretically, one may set up a theological course in which no interaction between students and instructors occurs. But while there may be certain courses in which this methodology is permissible, as a rule theological education is better done in formats with greater social presence.

6. An ideal approach to theological education would be to choose the format most effective at facilitating learning in a given situation. Paul employed a cohesive strategy for fulfilling his apostolic mission—a strategy that at times necessitated the dispatching of emissaries or the sending of letters. Occasionally, the sending of the letter was done on account of his conviction that it would promote his apostolic mission better than an apostolic visit. Likewise, theological institutions would do well to match the educational format appropriately with the learning objectives of courses. Some courses may lend themselves better to online formats than others. For example, a systematics or history course may lend itself to online formats better than a homiletics course, since homiletics involves preaching before live congregations.

7. Within hybrid formats, face-to-face elements might be employed most effectively toward the beginning of the course or program. This application stems from Paul's strategy of exercising his apostolic mission. That is, Paul tended to appeal to his former visits within his letters and through his emissaries. While some of his letters prepared the way for Paul to visit congregations he had never before visited, such as Romans, in general the epistles appeal to what congregations had heard and seen in him in his previous visits (1 Cor 4:16–17; 1 Thess 3:4). One of the means by which Paul sought to exert authority through his epistles was by arousing a sense in his hearers that he "appeared to be practically perceptible to the senses." He sought to arouse this sense by appealing to his audience's memory of him.[40] Likewise, putting face-to-face elements toward the beginning of hybrid courses or programs increases the social presence within online elements.

---

40 Jane M. F. Heath, "Absent Presences of Paul and Christ: *Enargeia* in 1 Thessalonians 1–3," *Journal for the Study of the New Testament* 32, no. 1 (2009): 4–5.

Recommendations for Contemporary Practice

Based upon the applications above, recommendations for practice are given:

1. Institutions should develop a clear strategy for utilizing various educational formats in carrying out their missions. Just as Paul used the visit, the letter, and the emissary as integral parts of a cohesive strategy for carrying out his apostolic mission, so also theological institutions should utilize various educational formats in a planned and deliberate way, consistent with their mission and ethos. This strategy will vary widely from institution to institution. An institution like Nashotah House Theological Seminary, in which daily Eucharist and prayer figure prominently in its ethos, will vary in approach from Rockbridge Seminary.[41] No matter what formats are utilized, they should be used in a clear and strategic way that is faithful to the mission and ethos of the institution.

2. Institutions that utilize online formats should equip faculty and students to facilitate social presence. Social presence helps to give legitimacy to online formats in theological education. Because social presence is so important, students and faculty should receive adequate preparation and resources to foster it. For example, faculty and students engaged in online formats might be required to receive training on why social presence is so important and how to foster social presence. Because social presence is so important, and because the face-to-face format provides more opportunities for the social than online formats, institutions utilizing online formats should strongly consider hybrid approaches. Strictly online formats and programs are also legitimate. But, the power of face-to-face communication should be strongly considered when planning programs and courses.

3. Institutions utilizing hybrid formats could effectively employ face-to-face elements toward the beginning of programs and courses. Based on Paul's example and the greater social bandwidth of face-to-face formats, this chapter argued that an appropriate application would be for hybrid formats to employ face-to-face elements toward

---

41 Nashotah House, "Daily Worship," accessed August 28, 2014, http://www.nashotah.edu/about/spiritual-formation/daily-worship/; Rockbridge Seminary, "About Rockbridge Online Seminary," accessed September 19, 2012, http://www.rockbridgeseminary.org/about-us.

the beginning of programs and courses. This recommendation might be carried out in many different ways. For example, a hybrid master of divinity program might include an intensive residency at the beginning of the program. Hybrid courses may include classroom portions at the beginning of the semester. In general, the research of this book suggests that students enrolled in the online portions of programs and courses will benefit from such early face-to-face interaction.

Conclusion

This chapter has not carried over all of the applications directly to practical recommendations. For example, one might expect a recommendation that master of divinity programs utilize hybrid approaches. Another recommendation that might be expected would be that ATS would continue its policy that accredited institutions require at least one year in residence, since it has been suggested that seminaries should emphasize face-to-face instruction. This chapter has not given such recommendations due to my conviction that, ideally, those responsible for decisions regarding the use of online formats in theological education should make these decisions not out of slavish adherence to specific recommendations but rather out of informed deliberation. Therefore, this chapter's most important recommendation is its first—that institutions develop a clear biblically and theologically grounded strategy for the ways that they choose to implement online education.

Opportunities for Application

Discover

> Analyze whether or not one's institution prioritizes face-to-face theological education.

Decide

> Determine where and how one's institution might be able to utilize face-to-face interaction to supplement online theological education.

Do

> Make plans for a pilot program to supplement online theological education with various forms of face-to-face interaction.

CHAPTER 4

Controversy and Common Ground

Chapters 2 and 3 offered guidance for online theological education on the basis of an analogical comparison to Pauline epistolary theory and practice. Those two chapters sit, however, within the context of a wider discussion of online theological education. This chapter will survey this discussion, and by this survey show the necessity of the two previous chapters. It will begin by examining theological arguments against the use of online formats in theological education. It will then analyze some of the weaker defenses of online theological education. Finally, this chapter will point out a key weakness in some of the stronger arguments against online theological education.

Concerns about Online Theological Education

Many opponents claim that online formats cannot accomplish the objectives of theological education. To examine the veracity of this claim, we must first outline what most believe to be those objectives.

Common Objectives in Theological Education

The objectives of theological education vary greatly between theological traditions and among institutions within those traditions. However, efforts have been made to promote a general standard. Most notable among these efforts are those of ATS, as found in their "Educational Standard" and "Degree Program Standards."[1] This document acknowledges the great diversity in educational approaches, yet promotes four general goals that should shape an institution's pedagogy and policies: "religious heritage, cultural context, personal and spiritual formation, and capacity for ministerial and public leadership."[2] Regarding religious heritage, institutions should seek to increase a student's identification with Christianity as a whole and his theological tradition in particular—a goal met primarily by the study of Scripture and history.[3] Understanding one's cultural context should help each student understand both the local and global character of the church. The goal of personal and spiritual formation is to help students mature in the Christian faith. As the standard indicates, "The program shall provide opportunities through which the student may grow in personal faith, emotional maturity, moral integrity, and public witness."[4] Most doubts concerning the capacities and appropriateness of online formats are associated with this area, because many believe spiritual formation is best achieved through residential education, as will be seen below. Finally, schools should foster a student's "capacity for ministerial and public leadership."[5]

ATS's "General Institutional, Educational, and Degree Program Standards" specify that the master of divinity should retain "at least one year of full-time academic study or its equivalent . . . at the main campus of the school awarding the degree or at an extension site of the institution."[6] ATS justifies this requirement based on their belief that strong student and faculty interaction is necessary to achieve the goals of the master of divinity degree.[7] Yet, ATS does allow for some

---

[1] Association of Theological Schools, "Educational Standard" and "Degree Program Standards," accessed May 30, 2017, http://www.ats.edu/uploads/accrediting/documents/accreditation-documents.pdf.
[2] Association of Theological Schools, "Degree Program Standards," A.2.1, http://www.ats.edu/uploads/accrediting/documents/accreditation-documents.pdf, accessed May 30, 2017.
[3] Ibid., A.2.2.1.
[4] Ibid., A.2.4, B.2.4, and C.2.1.3.
[5] Ibid., A.1.2.1.
[6] Ibid., A.3.1.3.
[7] Ibid.

exceptions, if an institution can demonstrate that the learning outcomes can be met without this residential period.[8]

Suspicion of Online Formats among Theological Educators

These "Educational and Degree Program Standards" indicate hesitation among theological educators to fully embrace online formats. Steve Delamarter gave documentary support of this hesitancy by surveying educators at forty-five theological institutions in the United States. He found repeated doubts regarding online theological education in three categories: practical and personal, pedagogical and educational, and philosophical and theological. Under each category, he includes actual comments from respondents. While Delamarter's practical and personal concerns are important, the other two categories are the most pertinent to this book. Pedagogical and educational concerns include the suspicion that a student might develop a fake online persona and therefore hinder the work of character formation that is considered to be part of theological education.[9] Educators were also concerned that the unique environment of face-to-face education, along with its spontaneity and open conversations, would be lost.[10] Some felt that certain courses like preaching were impossible to teach online, and others contended that theological education as a whole was not suitable to being taught online.[11]

Delamarter's reported concerns become even more pronounced within the philosophical and theological category. He explains that many theological educators thought that mentoring, character development, and spiritual formation were impossible to accomplish online.[12] Others claimed that since theological education is primarily focused on training ministers who will bring together communities, theological education should occur in community.[13] Respondents appealed to the

---

8   Ibid.
9   Steve Delamarter, "Theological Educators and Their Concerns about Technology," *Teaching Theology and Religion* 8, no. 3 (2005): 135.
10 Ibid., 135–36.
11 Ibid., 136.
12 Ibid., 137.
13 Ibid., 138.

words "incarnation" and "incarnational," arguing that community is central to Christianity.[14]

David Diekema and David Caddell published an article entitled, "The Significance of Place: Sociological Reflections on Distance Learning and Christian Higher Education," several years before Delamarter's article. The article describes the concerns many have with the use of online formats in Christian education, including those later outlined by Delamarter. First, the authors argue that the use of online formats does not allow for the same character formation that they believe occurs within residential educational programs.[15] Second, they fear that the use of online formats is not consistent with the personal, intimate education experience as commended by a personal God:

> Is not the incarnation of Jesus Christ ultimately God's rejection of distance learning? If relationship was an unnecessary component, would Christ's physical manifestation have been necessary? . . . Distance learning is not simply bad sociology, it is also inherently less than effective in assisting the Christian college or university to fulfill its mission.[16]

In other words, they believe that a commitment to residential education flows from a core doctrine of the Christian faith: the incarnation. Of course, Diekema and Caddell do not completely rule out the use of online formats in Christian education. But they do believe that the online formats should play a supporting role to Christian liberal arts education as traditionally understood.[17]

The Theological Argument against Online Theological Education

Delamarter suggests that philosophical and theological concerns may cause schools to completely opt out of online theological education.[18] Such has been argued by Paul House and Beeson Divinity School, where House is a professor of Old Testament. House has been one of the most

---

14   Ibid.
15   David Diekema and David Caddell, "The Significance of Place: Sociological Reflections on Distance Learning and Christian Higher Education," *Christian Scholar's Review* 31, no. 2 (2001): 171–79.
16   Ibid., 182.
17   Ibid., 169.
18   Ibid., 138.

vocal and eloquent opponents of online theological education, and the theological questions he has raised have kept Beeson from offering any online courses leading toward a degree.[19]

In the Spring 2010 edition of *Colloquy*, the semiannual publication of ATS, House makes a theological argument against online theological education. He contends that online theological education is inappropriate principally because the Scriptures commend face-to-face, intimate educational experiences:

> God sent his Son, not just his Word. Moses, Elijah, Huldah, Jesus, Barnabas, Paul, Aquila, and Priscilla mentored future servants of God. They did so face-to-face in community settings. They did so individually and in groups. They ate together. They prayed and worshiped God together. They suffered and shared together.[20]

House does admit that the writers of Scripture utilized other mediums, such as letters, but he explains that these were used to supplement face-to-face interaction.

House expands on these thoughts in his book, *Bonhoeffer's Seminary Vision: A Case for Costly Discipleship and Life Together*.[21] This book explores Dietrich Bonhoeffer's theology and practice of theological education and then applies his insights to today. Bonhoeffer emphasized what House calls "the biblical necessity of personal, incarnational, face-to-face education."[22] In the process of outlining Bonhoeffer's seminary vision, he also offers criticism of many contemporary trends in theological education, including the use of online formats. Three such criticisms are taken up below.

Committed students. According to House, Bonhoeffer's work demonstrates that God calls for theological students that are "completely

---

19 Beeson Divinity School, "FAQs about Beeson," accessed September 19, 2012, http://beesondivinity.com/faqsaboutbeeson; idem, "A Biblical Pattern for Theological Education," accessed September 19, 2012, http://beesondivinity.com/abiblicalpatternfortheologicaleducation.
20 House, "Hewing to Scripture's Pattern," 2, 6.
21 Idem, *Bonhoeffer's Seminary Vision: A Case for Costly Discipleship and Life Together* (Wheaton, IL: Crossway, 2015).
22 Ibid., 29.

committed to Christ and his calling in their lives."[23] House believes this kind of commitment is not encouraged by online formats:

> Programs marketed as easy to take and easy to gain do not sound much like what Bonhoeffer describes Jesus as teaching in the Sermon on the Mount. Programs that treat students as consumers instead of obedient servant followers of Christ hardly fit what Matthew 9:35–10:42 depicts. Where personal shaping of disciples diminishes or disappears, so does Christ's way of shaping shepherds.[24]

Incarnational seminaries of the visible body of Christ. House also believes that Bonhoeffer's view of the body of Christ as a visible entity militates against the idea of online theological education. For Bonhoeffer,

> the church will always be the body of Christ on earth until Jesus comes again. As such the church is the visible bodily form of Jesus, who took on human form to minister to human beings (see John 1:1–18; Phil. 2:5–11). It is visible wherever Christians live alone, with others, or in families, and wherever they meet in congregations or do any other individual or shared work. Christ's body is incarnational and relational by definition, according to Bonhoeffer. This understanding of the body of Christ extends to that body's work in Christian education, especially Christian education that forms the next generation of shepherds for God's people.[25]

That extension of the body of Christ to theological education, House contends, would exclude online formats, or any other format that cuts Christians off from each other, except in emergency situations.[26]

Addressing objections. House also deals with some objections to his viewpoint. One is the view that epistles serve as models for distance

---

23 Ibid., 89.
24 Ibid., 94.
25 Ibid., 98–99.
26 Ibid.

theological education.[27] House argues that the comparison does not hold up under closer scrutiny:[28]

> The Epistles were not sent to lone individuals who then read them in private. They were addressed to individuals and congregations. They were each carried not by a government employee, but by one or more Christians sent from the apostle. These carriers were there to discuss the contents, explain the apostle's situation, and share fellowship with the recipients. Thus, these letters embodied a relationship already begun. Even in a letter like the one to the Romans, whom Paul had not visited yet, the apostle takes great pains to connect to the recipients through people known to both parties and through the ones bringing the letter. So one would be on firmer ground to argue that the correlation between use of electronic communication and the Epistles is one of supporting current relationships between known parties. Even then, the carrier of the letter is missing. The incarnational element is truncated at best, absent at worst.[29]

Misplaced Defenses

Those most opposed to online theological education, like House, Diekema, and Caddell, base their objections in philosophical and theological concerns. On the other hand, those countering such concerns often respond with pragmatic justifications lacking in theological depth.

For example, in a counterpoint article to House's "Hewing to Scripture's Pattern," Meri MacLeod gives no defense of online theological education grounded in theological or biblical reflection. She simply enumerates the strategic benefits for theological schools pursuing online theological education—such as learning-centered course design and student assessment, the facilitating of student body diversity, and

---

[27] Ibid., 188.
[28] Ibid.
[29] Ibid., 185–86.

the preparation of students well adapted to the technological demands of present-day ministry.[30]

This lack of theological reflection is also demonstrated in a response to Diekema and Caddell's article by Van B. Weigel. He justifies his position by citing ways in which online formats can enrich the educational experience.[31] Such benefits include the opportunity to rearrange learning sequences more easily according to different educational models.[32] While online formats may indeed offer such an opportunity, arguments like his do not answer the fundamental philosophical and theological concerns held by Diekema and Caddell. Both Weigel and MacLeod offer a pragmatic defense to theological objections.[33]

Attempted Theological and Biblical Justifications of Online Formats

Those who have attempted a theological defense of online theological education have typically pursued two lines of argument. Some have sought to demonstrate that the desired outcomes of theological education in general, as described for example in ATS's "Educational and Degree Program Standards," do actually occur through online theological education. They maintain that even the spiritual formation of students can be done through an online format. For instance, Maddix and Estep promote the idea that spiritual development can

---

30 Meri MacLeod, "The Case for Distance Learning in Theological Education: Six Strategic Benefits of Interactive Web-Based Distance Learning," *Colloquy* 18, no. 2 (2010): 7.
31 Van B. Weigel, "Reflection: Place in the Digital Age: Familiar Dichotomies No Longer Apply," *Christian Scholar's Review* 32, no. 1 (2002): 14–18.
32 Ibid., 14–16.
33 For other examples of those who base their support for online theological education primarily on pragmatic grounds, see Stephen Haar, "E-Constructing Theological Education for Ministry in a www World," *Lutheran Theological Journal* 42, no. 1 (May 2008): 18–29; M. E. Hess, "Attending to Embodiedness in Online, Theologically Focused Learning" (paper presented at Going the Distance: Theology, Religious Education, and Interactive Distance Education, University of Dayton, 1999); MacLeod, "The Case for Distance Learning"; Matthew C. Ogilvie, "Teaching Theology Online," *Australian EJournal of Theology* 13, no. 1 (2009): 66.

occur within online environments. This spiritual development is best achieved with personal skills, such as Bible study, and less successful with intrinsically communal practices (church worship, for example).[34] Lowe examines whether or not students feel that they have developed spiritually through online courses.[35] Her conclusion is in the affirmative, but her study has two weaknesses. First, it measures only student reactions. Students may feel like they have experienced spiritual formation without actually having experienced it. Second, it does not answer the question as to whether or not spiritual formation from a distance is theologically permissible.

A second, more promising line of argument comes from Forrest and Lamport. They argue that in Romans, Paul attempted to promote spiritual growth among his readers from a distance.[36] This line of inquiry goes a long way in answering the objections of those who are concerned with online theological education, as it shows that Paul himself believed that spiritual and theological formation could occur over a distance. While their article does not answer all the objections of the critics of online theological education, their method of bringing Paul to bear on online theological education was expanded upon in this book's previous two chapters.

A number of other writers have also sought to justify online theological education through biblical and theological arguments. For instance, Esselman argues that the New Testament presents a communal and egalitarian vision for theological learning and that online formats actually reflect this vision better than traditional formats. According to Esselman, the New Testament envisions theological learning occurring within "wisdom communities," within which knowledge would be discovered, shared, and received.[37] He then argues that

---

34 Mark A. Maddix and James Riley Estep, "Spiritual Formation in Online Higher Education Communities: Nurturing Spirituality in Christian Higher Education Online Degree Programs," *Christian Education Journal* 7, no. 2 (September 1, 2010): 429, 433.

35 Mary Lowe, "A Summary of the Findings of the Study: Assessing the Impact of Online Courses on the Spiritual Formation of Adult Students," *Christian Perspectives in Education* 4, no. 1 (Fall 2010): 1–18.

36 Benjamin K. Forrest and Mark A. Lamport, "Modeling Spiritual Formation from a Distance: Paul's Formation Transactions with the Roman Christians," *Christian Education Journal* 10 (2013): 110–24.

37 Thomas Esselman, "The Pedagogy of the Online Wisdom Community:

online theological education closely corresponds to this model given that it tends to be less focused on the transmission of knowledge from one person to a group, as is often the case in the traditional classroom. On the contrary, the group pursues knowledge together, with the instructor taking a more facilitating role.[38] Esselman's work establishes that online formats effectively facilitate the formation of wisdom communities. However, it fails to give the biblical and theological founding of online education needed to justify it to those who so strongly object to it. First, Esselman does not prove that the New Testament advocates the formation of wisdom communities. Admittedly, he cites many secondary sources that make this claim, but it is little more than a hypothesis. The only concrete example he gives of a biblical wisdom community is the group gathered at the Last Supper, a face-to-face gathering.[39] Esselman's work is therefore unlikely to persuade those who, for theological concerns, oppose the use of online formats in theological education.

Gresham offers perhaps the most compelling theological justification for online theological education, though some aspects of his argument are stronger than others. For the sake of brevity, we will focus on his strongest point—namely, that God's self-disclosure has always been adaptive and accommodating and has made use of rich signs and symbols.[40] Based on this reality, Gresham concludes that it is in keeping with the character of God to embrace online theological education, which is an adaptation to the digitalized culture of today, and which allows for the use of a great variety of media: videos, music, images, and the like.[41]

Conclusion

In conclusion, many of those who have attempted philosophical and theological arguments for online theological education have depended

---

Forming Church Ministers in a Digital Age," *Teaching Theology & Religion* 7, no. 3 (2004): 164–65.

[38] Ibid., 167–69.
[39] Ibid., 164.
[40] John Gresham, "The Divine Pedagogy as a Model for Online Education," *Teaching Theology & Religion* 9, no. 1 (2006): 25.
[41] Ibid., 25–26.

on questionable premises. While a few authors, most notably Gresham and Forrest and Lamport, have pursued some promising arguments, their arguments do not rise to a full defense of online theological education against its strongest critics. Beyond this, their arguments, as promising as they are as defenses of online theological education, give little by way of guidance for online theological education. This is why this book's previous two chapters are necessary. As this survey of pertinent literature shows, a stronger theological grounding for online theological education has been sorely needed.

But does this book's previous two chapters accomplish a defense of online theological education? Do they meet the strongest objections against the use of online formats, most notably those of Paul House? The following paragraphs will not offer a full rebuttal of House's claims. Indeed, as House's argument is an analogical one, full rebuttal is not possible as it would be with deductive arguments. Therefore, I will show that the analogical comparison I have made is a stronger one than House's. I do this with fear and trembling, since I find the vision of theological education envisioned by Bonhoeffer and in turn by House quite appealing and compelling. My own ministerial formation was a model of the kind of education for which House advocates. I often say that I learned as much theology singing in seminary choir as I did in exegetics or systematics classes. And yet, I contend that House has overstated his case.

House's argument for what he calls in-the-flesh theological education is not based on necessity. He does not argue deductively, showing the logical necessity of his vision of in-the-flesh theological education. House compares on the one hand such phenomena as the self-revelation of God and Jesus's vision of disciple formation and on the other hand theological education; from these comparisons he then draws conclusions regarding how to accomplish theological formation.

House is not wrong to present an analogical argument. Chapters 1 and 2 of this book also argue by way of analogy. However, this book's analogical argument is stronger than House's analogical argument. Therefore, the conclusions of this book are more plausible than the conclusions that House makes.

At this point, perhaps it would be helpful to review the guidelines for evaluating the strength of analogical arguments:

> The more similarities (between two domains), the stronger the analogy . . .
> The more differences, the weaker the analogy . . .
> The greater the extent of our ignorance about the two domains, the weaker the analogy . . .
> The weaker the conclusion, the more plausible the analogy.[42]

House's main objections to online theological education stem from a comparison between the domains of God's incarnational self-revelation and the domain of theological education. House compares the incarnation of the Son of God and the Son's continued incarnational presence in the world by means of the church with theological education. By way of contrast, the domains that I have compared have to do with Pauline epistolography and theological education.

The analogy that I have offered is preferable, in part, on account of the domains I have sought to compare. There are far more similarities and fewer differences between Pauline epistolography and theological education than there are between God's incarnational self-disclosure and theological education. The incarnational immanence of the transcendent God in Christ and in Christ's body, the church, is one of the mysteries of Christian faith, a truth that can be apprehended but not comprehended. Christians know that it has happened, for they have such signs as prophecy, eyewitness testimony of the resurrection and ascension, Jesus's testimony that he will always be with the church, and other such signs that testify to God's incarnational immanence. And yet, ultimately the truth of the incarnation, that the infinite took on finiteness, that the eternal entered into time, that the Creator became a part of creation, defies comprehension.

Such inability to comprehend the incarnation stems from human inability to comprehend the domain of the divine. As finite beings, we can speak about infinity, but we cannot fully understand infinity. As part of creation, in which nothing is made without existing matter or energy, God's creation out of nothing lies outside human experience. The domain of the divine so lies outside of human knowledge that theologians have often depended on analogies from the domain of the created world in order to describe it. Even God's incarnational presence

---

42 Bartha, "Analogy and Analogical Reasoning."

through the church is a mystery, so that theologians often describe it as an article of faith. House's analogy is, therefore, quite weak, insofar as he seeks to render judgments on the domain of theological education based upon the domain of the incarnation, a domain that lies largely beyond human knowledge. The analogy I have presented is stronger, because it is based on the known domain of Pauline epistolography.

This analogy is also to be preferred because the conclusions I have drawn are more modest than the conclusions drawn by House and therefore more plausible. From his analogy, House concludes that online theological education should never be pursued, except in extremely marginal cases. From my analogy, I have suggested that online education is permissible within a deliberate educational approach that takes into account an institution's mission and ethos as well as the relative merits of an online format or face-to-face format.

In sum, much of the past debate surrounding online theological education has been severely lacking. The critics of online theological education who base their criticisms upon theological concerns have frequently appealed to weak arguments. Attempted justifications of online theological education have either relied upon pragmatic considerations or, if they have taken up theological concerns, have also presented weak arguments. My hope is that these three chapters have forged a better path, providing more robust theological foundations for discussions of online theological education than we have previously seen.

Opportunities for Application

Discover

    Analyze the theological foundations for resistance to online theological education in one's institution.

Decide

    Determine to seek and to follow a biblical model for theological education, regardless of cost or convenience.

Do

    Carefully study House's critique of online theological education and consider which of his arguments are strongest and which are weakest.

Section II
Better Faculty for Online Learning

How Strong Theological Foundations Can Improve Online Faculty

Gabriel Etzel

I do not remember my exact words to the staff member working in the School of Religion at the time, but it was something to the effect of, "We need to hire one hundred online faculty members over the next twelve months." At the time, the institution where I serve was experiencing unprecedented growth in our online division, and I was attempting to get in front of the large tsunami of future enrollment. Over the next year, we fell slightly short of the hiring goal (we hired somewhere around eighty online faculty during the year). But the daunting task of recruiting, hiring, training, deploying, and developing on average two online faculty members per week for an entire year caused our department to think strategically about our online faculty hiring practices. From interviews, to processing of employee files, to deployment, to development, we needed to make sure we were intentional about our actions. Our students' education was at stake, and we were not willing to fail.

Other institutions may not need to hire one hundred faculty members in the period of twelve months, but I am convinced that no matter what the size of an institution or department, the principles of hiring and developing faculty remain the same. The importance of having the right faculty member overseeing an online course is hard to overstate, and the process of faculty hiring, training, deployment, and development should be undertaken with deeply rooted theological convictions.

This section will argue that the faculty member in the context of online theological education should not be seen primarily as "a sage on the stage" or a "guide on the side," but rather, the online faculty member should be seen as a model to follow. This understanding of the faculty being a model to follow will then direct the hiring, training, deployment, and development of those faculty members. In the next chapter, I will argue that humanity's creation in the image of God makes it imperative that online theological training prioritizes the formation of the student over information transfer. In the subsequent chapter, faculty hiring will be discussed. I will contend that when hiring, institutions must prioritize the theological competencies of applicants, in the form of spiritual development and formation, ahead of technological and pedagogical competencies, as is evidenced by the example provided by the apostle Paul to follow him as he follows Christ. In chapter 7, faculty development and training will be considered. I will stress that the institution should foster the online faculty member's ongoing spiritual formation as a modeler of Christ. This is seen in the ongoing life and ministry of the apostle Paul, who demonstrated Christian character and formation throughout his ministry.

CHAPTER 5

Online Faculty and the Image of God

No more important role exists in Christian higher education than that of the Christian faculty member. As Gaebelein writes, "The school or college that would develop a Christ-centered and biblically grounded program must fly from its mast this standard, 'No Christian education without Christian teachers,' and must never under any conditions pull its colors down."[1] Thus, an institution must be intentional about the type of faculty member they hire for teaching online courses. As has been argued in the previous section of this work, the impact of the faculty member's social presence within the online classroom can have a dramatic effect on the spiritual development of students.

However, being present within the classroom is not enough. The faculty member must be present in a way that demonstrates one's own formation into the image of Christ and promotes the formation of the student. As such, educators must have a clear understanding of the goal of spiritual formation, which is formation into the image of Christ. Forrest and Lamport state,

> Spiritual formation, we contend, is the process of coming to grips with our finite humanness and developing an

---

1   Frank E. Gaebelein, *The Pattern of God's Truth* (Whittier, CA: Association of Christian Schools International, 1968), 37.

understanding that our sufficiency lies in the person of Christ. This definition represents the "transformed mind" that Paul describes in Romans 12. The result of this type of transformation is an understanding that our position and sufficiency are wholly and completely dependent upon Christ and what he has completed for us in his death and resurrection.[2]

This understanding of formation has important implications for the role of the faculty member. In the following chapter, I will argue that the primary implication of this view of formation is that the role of the faculty member must move beyond being merely a guide for students throughout the learning process. Instead, faculty must model spiritual formation for their students.

> **Spiritual Formation**
>
> The process of the Christian becoming more conformed to the image of Christ.

Theological Anthropology and Pedagogy

Online theological training is an intersection of theology, pedagogy, and technology. Because education is about both curriculum and the student, an educator should develop an awareness of theological anthropology's influence on pedagogy (which is the how and why of teaching).[3] In his work *Desiring the Kingdom*, James K. A. Smith argues that behind every pedagogy is a view of theological anthropology.[4] By this it is understood that the way in which we view humanity will influence and shape the way we educate others. For instance, educational theories based on an understanding that mankind is at the core a thinking being will focus the educational system on the dissemination of information.[5] On the other hand, educational theories that believe

---

2   Benjamin K. Forrest and Mark A. Lamport, "Modeling Spiritual Formation from a Distance: Paul's Formation Transactions with the Roman Christians," *Christian Education Journal* 10, no. 1 (2013): 111.
3   In response to the question "What do teachers teach?" Neil Postman states, "Teachers teach subjects." By this he means that teachers teach both students (subjects) and content (subjects).
4   James K. A. Smith, *Desiring the Kingdom: Worship, Worldview, and Cultural Formation* (Grand Rapids: Baker Academic, 2009), 27, 45.
5   Ibid., 28.

mankind is a desiring being will focus on forming the desires of the individual.[6] Therefore, online educators should have a firm grasp on what it means to be human, which from a biblical perspective is centered on humanity's creation in the image of God.

> **Theological Anthropology**
>
> The study of humanity, especially in relationship to God.

The Concept of the Image of God

A proper understanding of the image of God is essential to a correct theological anthropology.[7] As such, the online educator must have a robust understanding of the image of God and its implications for theological anthropology in order to grasp properly the role of the online faculty member. In the following section, the biblical teachings on the image of God are presented, followed by an overview of the historical understanding of the doctrine. Finally, the concept is further explored using Psalm 8 as a lens to interpret the nature of mankind's creation in the image of God. This study will demonstrate that for the Christian educator, Christ should define and determine what spiritual formation looks like in the life of the believer, as Christ is the perfect image of God (Col 1:15; Heb 1:3) and as Christians are being transformed into his image (Rom 12:1–2).

Biblical Teaching on Imago Dei

The first reference to mankind's creation in the image of God is found in Genesis 1:26. Even a casual reading of Genesis 1 reveals the contrast between the events of days 1–5 and day 6. Something out of the ordinary occurs with the creation of humanity in Genesis 1. Indeed, the entire text of Genesis 2 is devoted to a further explanation of the events of day 6. Nahum Sarna concludes, "A human being is the pinnacle of Creation."[8] As recorded in Scripture, the following words culminate the creation account:

---

6   The premise behind Smith's work is that at the core humans are desiring beings. This will be explored later.
7   Michael F. Bird, *Evangelical Theology: A Biblical and Systematic Introduction* (Grand Rapids: Zondervan, 2013), 657.
8   Nahum M. Sarna, *Genesis*, JPS Torah Commentary (Philadelphia: Jewish Publication Society of America, 1989), 11.

> Then God said, "Let us make man in our image, after our likeness. And let them have dominion over the fish of the sea and over the birds of the heavens and over the livestock and over all the earth and over every creeping thing that creeps on the earth." So God created man in his own image, in the image of God he created him; male and female he created them. (Gen 1:26–27)

The meaning of "image" and "likeness." An investigation into the meaning of the words "image" and "likeness" used in Genesis 1:26–27 helps to determine the words' theological significance. Westermann argues that "image" can mean a statue, as in 2 Chronicles 23:17, or an image of the gods, as in Ezekiel 7:20.[9] In a similar way, the meaning of "likeness" is well established. As noted by von Rad, "'Likeness' is a verbal abstraction and means predominantly something abstract: 'appearance,' 'similarity,' or 'analogy.'"[10] The meanings "image" and "likeness" establish the importance of mankind's creation, yet questions remain as to whether or not the words are synonymous within the context of mankind's creation.

Although commentators continue to debate whether "image" and "likeness" are interchangeable, both words are used in Genesis 1:26 and Genesis 5:3, which indicates there is significance to both words being used. In commenting on the meanings of image and likeness, Gentry notes that "likeness" speaks to Adam being a son of God, and "image" speaks to Adam being a "servant king."[11] As such, Gentry's understanding is that both words are to be interpreted in reference to relationship. Skinner also supports a distinction between "image" and "likeness," yet concludes that likeness to God is not something actually realized within creation.[12] Gentry opposes Keil and Delitzsch, who conclude that the two words are used interchangeably.[13] Among those

---

9   Claus Westermann, *Genesis 1–11*, Continental Commentary (Minneapolis: Fortress, 1994), 146.
10   Gerhard von Rad, *Genesis*, Old Testament Library (Louisville: Westminster John Knox, 1973), 57–58.
11   Peter Gentry, "Kingdom through Covenant," *The Southern Baptist Journal of Theology* 12, no. 1 (2008): 28–29.
12   John Skinner, *Genesis*, International Critical Commentary (Edinburgh: T & T Clark, 1910), 32.
13   C. F. Keil and Franz Delitzsch, *Pentateuch*, Commentary on the Old Testament,

agreeing with Keil and Delitzsch are Wenham[14] and Collins;[15] however, the fact that several passages use both "image" and "likeness" indicates a significance to both words being used. "Image" and "likeness" appear to represent two connected, yet distinct, relationships—mankind's relationship to God, and mankind's relationship to God's creation. For the Christian educator, the importance of a relationship with God and with others within the context of spiritual formation is essential, as the goal of spiritual formation is becoming more Christlike. The biblical teachings on the image of God remind the online educator that both the online faculty member and the online students have value and purpose, and both have a responsibility to foster relationships with God and others.

Historical Understandings of the Imago Dei

Within the modern era, biblical commentators and theologians have attempted to explain the essence of mankind's creation in the image of God.[16] Five primary views are presented as possible explanations for the image of God.[17] The substantival view indicates that humans possess attributes or characteristics of God; imageness is something the human is. Those who hold the functional view assert that imageness is something that a human *does*. The relational view focuses on a human being's relationship with God or others. The teleological view speaks of

---

    vol. 1 (Grand Rapids: Eerdmans, 1975), 63.

14 Gordon J. Wenham, *Genesis 1–15*, vol. 1, Word Biblical Commentary (Nashville: Thomas Nelson, 1987), 30.

15 C. John Collins, *Genesis 1–4: A Linguistic, Literary, and Theological Commentary* (Phillipsburg, NJ: P & R Publishing, 2006), 62.

16 Westermann, *Genesis 1–11*, 148–53; Wenham, *Genesis 1–15*, 1:29–32.

17 Millard Erickson arranges the views under three headings: substantive, relational, and functional; however, Gregg Allison and James Estep divide the various views into four categories: substantival, functional, relational, and teleological, and Michael Bird presents various views including the royal view. Millard J. Erickson, *Christian Theology*, 2nd ed. (Grand Rapids: Baker Academic, 1998); James R. Estep, Michael Anthony, and Greg Allison, *A Theology for Christian Education* (Nashville: B&H Academic, 2008); James R. Estep and Jonathan H. Kim, eds., *Christian Formation: Integrating Theology and Human Development* (Nashville: B&H Academic, 2010); Bird, *Evangelical Theology*.

the destiny of humans.[18] The royal view "means that humanity is royal and is created to rule."[19]

Historically, the nature and identification of the image of God has generated much discussion. In general, scholarship supports that mankind's creation in the image of God indicates that mankind is unique among God's creation. In addition, most theologians throughout church history believe that the image of God remained within humanity after the fall of mankind as recorded in Genesis 3. Although numerous theories are presented within scholarship as to the precise meaning of the image of God, many commentators note that the concept of the image of God has implications for humanity's relationship to both God and God's creation. The concept also has important implications for online educators within the context of graduate-level ministerial training.

The Imago Dei *in Its Ancient Near-Eastern Historical Context*

A review of the biblical and historical context pertaining to mankind's creation in the image of God would not be complete without also considering the ancient Near-Eastern context of Genesis. Gentry presents a compelling argument related to the historical significance of the idea of an "image" in the ancient Near-Eastern world. Gentry stresses that imageness is not physical appearance. Rather, those bearing the image of the gods in the ancient Near-Eastern context behaved like the gods. He concludes that within this context, the image of God would "communicate two main ideas: (1) rulership and (2) sonship."[20] Similarly, Sarna notes that in contrast to a ruling monarch bearing the image of God alone in other ancient Near-Eastern cultures, from a biblical perspective, "each person bears the stamp of royalty."[21] Thus, humans share equal dignity before God and with each other, as they rule over God's creation. This relatedness to God and to creation carries relevance for online graduate-level ministerial training, as the nature of this training is interaction with God, with others, and with God's creation. How educators perceive students (even at a distance)

---

18   Estep, Anthony, and Allison, *A Theology for Christian Education*, 179–80.
19   Bird, *Evangelical Theology*, 659.
20   Gentry, "Kingdom through Covenant," 27.
21   Sarna, *Genesis*, 12.

and how students view others correlate with the understanding of image of God.

The Imago Dei: Son-ship and Ruler-ship

Based on the use of "image" throughout the Old Testament, the *imago Dei* is at times interpreted as a physical representation of God on earth. Gentry stresses the physical aspect, but notes that the image "goes far beyond being merely physical,"[22] which is important for online educators to consider as most of their interactions will not be face-to-face. This interpretation that the image of God consists of both physical and spiritual attributes is supported by a number of scholars.[23] The divine edict against murder in Genesis 9:6 also supports an understanding of the physical aspect of the image of God, because it is an edict against the abuse of the physical aspect of man. Many other references to the *imago Dei* in Scripture are in the context of a physical manifestation (e.g., Christ as revealing the invisible Father in John 14:9 and Col 1:15), or of the exercising of dominion (Psalm 8; 1 Cor 11:7; Col 1:15–20). Westermann and Wenham each provide an overview of positions.[24] Many commentators also address the question of dominion, and although David Cotter suggests the image *is* mankind's ability to have dominion,[25] most commentaries propose that the exercising of dominion is a *result* of mankind being created in the image of God, and not the image itself.[26]

---

22 Gentry, "Kingdom through Covenant," 32.
23 Skinner, *Genesis*, 12; von Rad, *Genesis*, 60; Hermann Gunkel et al., *Genesis* (Macon, GA: Mercer University Press, 1997), 113; Sarna, *Genesis*, 12. This view is rejected by Keil and Delitzsch, who instead view the image of God to consist "in the spiritual personality of man" (Keil and Delitzsch, *Pentateuch*, I:63–64). William Reyburn and Euan Fry suggest the image of God is both spiritual and physical. (William D. Reyburn and Euan McG. Fry, *A Handbook on Genesis*, UBS Handbooks [New York: United Bible Societies, 1997], 50.)
24 Westermann, *Genesis 1–11*, 148–53; Wenham, *Genesis 1–15*, 1:29–32.
25 David W. Cotter, *Genesis*, Berit Olam (Collegeville, MN: Michael Glazier, 2003), 18.
26 Umberto Cassuto, *From Adam to Noah: A Commentary on the Book of Genesis I–VI* (Jerusalem: Magnes Press, Hebrew University, 1978), 58; Keil and Delitzsch, *Pentateuch*, I:64; Skinner, *Genesis*, 32; von Rad, *Genesis*, 59; Wenham, *Genesis 1–15*, 1:32; Westermann, *Genesis 1–11*, 153.

In attempting to conclude what humanity's creation in the image of God means, Hamilton notes, "Any approach that focuses on one aspect of man—be that physical, spiritual, or intellectual—to the neglect of the rest of man's constituent features seems doomed to failure."[27] Allison likewise challenges any view that would "reduce the image of God to one particular part or aspect of our humanness."[28] Additionally, Millard Erickson indicates,

> The image is something in the very nature of humans, in the way they were made. It refers to something a human *is* rather than something a human *has* or *does*. By virtue of being human, one is in the image of God; it is not dependent upon the presence of anything else.[29]

Hoekema and Gentry have similar conclusions concerning the image of God. Hoekema states, "The image of God . . . describes not just something that man *has*, but something man *is*."[30] Gentry expresses this view again within the context of his discussion on the man being created *in* the image of God. Gentry indicates, "Man *is* the divine image."[31] Gentry and Wellum also explain that creation in the image of God "defines a divine-human relationship" with a vertical and a horizontal dimension.[32] Mankind rules over God's creation as a result of being created in the image of God, but that ruling is not the essence of the divine image.[33] Sarna proposes that the image of God is "the symbol of God's presence on earth."[34] These are different interpretations and explanations of what it means to be created in the image of God. In the context of online education, the importance of the image of God relates to all aspects of humanity (physical, spiritual, emotional, intellectual, volitional). The educator and the student should recognize the

---

27 Hamilton, *The Book of Genesis, Chapters 1–17*, 137.
28 Estep, Anthony, and Allison, *A Theology for Christian Education*, 180.
29 Erickson, *Christian Theology*, 532.
30 Anthony A. Hoekema, *Created in God's Image* (Grand Rapids: Eerdmans, 1986), 95.
31 Gentry, "Kingdom through Covenant," 32.
32 Peter John Gentry and Stephen J. Wellum, *Kingdom through Covenant: A Biblical-Theological Understanding of the Covenants* (Wheaton, IL: Crossway, 2012), 200.
33 Ibid., 200–201.
34 Sarna, *Genesis*, 12.

image of God in one another and acknowledge their responsibility and relationship to God, to others, and to God's creation.

In summary, the image of God is the condition in which humanity was created. It does not specify a single quality, but rather, speaks of the person as a whole. Genesis 9:6 makes it clear that the image of God remained after the fall of man, and after the flood, as does James 3:9. Mankind relates to God and to others as a result of being created in the image of God. This concept is also the foundation from which mankind exercises dominion over the rest of God's creation. Mankind is the representation of God to the rest of creation, neither taking away the significance of God's rightful place of supremacy, nor denying the general revelation of God as revealed throughout the rest of his creation. Because of the image of God, humanity serves as God's vice-regent on earth, in order to accomplish God's desires for God's creation.

> **Image of God**
>
> The condition in which humanity was created in order to represent God to God's creation, and which allows humanity to enter into relationships with God, each other, and God's creation.

Humanity's creation in the image of God, and the resulting relationship to God, to others, and to creation is an important foundation from which the online educator can train students. Indeed, the role of the faculty member is influenced by the recognition of the dignity and relationship inherent within humanity. In addition, humanity's God-given position of dominion over God's creation is a direct result of humanity's creation in the image of God.

Example of Psalm 8: The Emphasis Is God

As significant as humanity's creation in the image of God is within the biblical narrative, ultimately, to be created in the image of God is not merely a statement about humanity, as though mankind was at the center of creation. Instead, it is a statement about God. As the psalmist reflects on the creation of mankind in Psalm 8, he is moved not by the greatness of man, but by the greatness of God. An adoration for God bookends the chapter: "O LORD, our Lord, how majestic is your name in all the earth!" Mankind is but a piece (albeit a significant piece) of God's creation.

This position of subservience is expounded further in verses 3–4, which read, "When I look at your heavens, the work of your fingers, the moon and the stars, which you have set in place, what is man that you are mindful of him, and the son of man that you care for him?" Based on this text, Craigie states that mankind's position is not innate to him, but rather God-given.[35] Similarly, Weiser mentions, "Face to face with God man becomes aware of the total insignificance of his existence."[36] Weiser proclaims it is not man's ability that leads to dominion over creation, but rather God's design.[37]

In a similar statement, Schaefer affirms both the image of God in Psalm 8, and the significance of God's sovereign rule over creation. Referencing Psalm 8, he contends that humanity should not be led to pride, but rather praise for the greatness of God.[38] Consequently, the point of reflecting on the *imago Dei* is not to exalt humanity; the point is to exalt God. The Bible is not a story of man and his works; it is the revelation of God, his action and interaction with his creation. The hero of the story is God, and the King on the throne is Jesus Christ. The glory of God should cause humanity to bow down in awe of their Creator and Sustainer. For the online educator, the ultimate purpose of the educational process should be to glorify God by prioritizing the student's formation into the image of God. Consequently, formation of the individual is not ultimately for the sake of the individual; but ultimately, the purpose of formation is for the glory of God. And as will be demonstrated within the next section of this chapter, this formation is only possible through the person and work of Christ (Col 1:15; Heb 1:3).

Jesus Christ, Image of God

The nature of mankind's creation in the image of God is further explained by considering the person of Christ. Speaking of Christ,

[35] Peter Craigie, *Psalms 1–50*, Word Biblical Commentary, vol. 19 (Waco, TX: Word, 1983), 107–8.
[36] Artur Weiser, *Psalms*, Old Testament Library (Louisville: Westminster John Knox, 1962), 143.
[37] Ibid., 144–45.
[38] Konrad Schaefer, *Psalms*, Berit Olam (Collegeville, MN: Liturgical, 2001).

Hebrews 1:3 calls Christ the "exact imprint" of God's nature, and Colossians 1:15 states that Jesus is the "image of the invisible God." In addition, Romans 8:29 states, "For those whom he foreknew he also predestined to be conformed to the image of his Son." Commenting on Romans 8:29, Hoekema concludes, "Since the Son, as we have just seen, is the perfect image of God the Father, we will not do violence to the text if we interpret the expression 'image of his Son' as being equivalent to 'image of God.'"[39] Christians are to be transformed into the image of Christ (2 Cor 3:18), which by extension, is formation into the correct image of God. Thus, the image of God is more than a defining aspect of theological anthropology;[40] it is a defining aspect of the Christian life. Within the context of online theological training, both the faculty member and the student have a responsibility to be formed into Christ's image. Theological training is for the purpose of preparing ministers to lead in the work of the ministry, and as such, these same students should learn to model and lead others within a congregation to be formed into the image of Christ.

Ware reminds his readers that humanity's relationship with God stands apart from any other relationship, and that humanity should allow God to define that relationship.[41] Colossians 1 speaks of Christ as being in the image of God, and then talks about his ruling over the world and holding the world together:

> He is the image of the invisible God, the firstborn over all creation. For everything was created by him, in heaven and on earth, the visible and the invisible, whether thrones or dominions or rulers or authorities—all things have been created through him and for him. He is before all things, and by him all things hold together. He is also the head of the body, the church; he is the beginning, the firstborn from the dead, so that he might come to have first place in everything. For God was pleased to have all his fullness dwell in him, and through him to reconcile everything to himself, whether things on earth or things in

---

39 Hoekema, *Created in God's Image*, 23.
40 Bird, *Evangelical Theology*, 657.
41 Bruce A. Ware, *God's Greater Glory: The Exalted God of Scripture and the Christian Faith* (Wheaton, IL: Crossway, 2004).

heaven, by making peace through his blood, shed on the cross. (Col 1:15–20 CSB)

Two words within the text deserve special consideration. First, the Greek word translated "image" in verse 15 raises questions. Dunn, Barth, and Blanke provide overviews of the Greek uses of "image" and arrive at conflicting conclusions concerning its interpretation.[42] Barth and Blanke conclude that the term "image" refers to Christ's relationship to all of creation, and not primarily to God the Father, due in large part to the combination of "image" with the "firstborn of all creation."[43] O'Brien disagrees with this interpretation and notes the significance of the fact that Paul only uses the word here and in 2 Corinthians 4:4 when referring to Christ. In addition, he states,

> The very nature and character of God have been perfectly revealed in him [Christ]; in him the invisible has become visible. Both Old and New Testaments make it plain that "no one has ever seen God." The Fourth Evangelist, however, adds that "the only begotten Son, who is in the bosom of the Father, has made him known" (John 1:18).[44]

O'Brien proceeds to indicate that the use of "image" in Colossians 1:15 is a title of majesty, emphasizing "Christ's relation to God."[45] Bruce agrees with O'Brien's assessment of the significance of Paul's usage of *image* in verse 15: "To say that Christ is the image of God is to say that in him the nature and being of God have been perfectly revealed—that in him the invisible has become visible."[46] The true image of God in visible form is the person of Jesus Christ. For the online educator who is often not in the same room with students,

---

42 James D. G. Dunn, *The Epistles to the Colossians and to Philemon*, New International Greek Testament Commentary (Grand Rapids: Eerdmans, 1996), 87–88.

43 Markus Barth and Helmut Blanke, *Colossians*, Anchor Bible (New Haven: Yale University Press, 1995), 195.

44 Peter T. O'Brien, *Colossians, Philemon*, vol. 44, Word Biblical Commentary (Nashville: Thomas Nelson, 1982), 43.

45 Ibid., 44.

46 F. F. Bruce, *The Epistles to the Colossians, to Philemon, and to the Ephesians*, New International Commentary on the New Testament (Grand Rapids: Eerdmans, 1984), 57–58.

knowing that conformity into the image of God involves more than a student's body is an important and refreshing reality.

The second phrase to be considered is "firstborn over all creation." The significance of the phrase has been debated by commentators. O'Brien argues, "If 'image' . . . emphasizes Christ's relation to God, then the second title, 'firstborn of all creation' . . . designates his relationship to the creation."[47] The word translated "firstborn" is a combination of the Greek word that means "first" with a term that means "chief." Hendriksen says of this phrase that Christ is "the One to whom belongs the right and dignity of the Firstborn in relation to every creature. . . . He is prior to, distinct from, and highly exalted above every creature."[48] Christ has a unique relationship with God the Father.

This is an important passage of Scripture as related to the person and work of Christ. Simpson comments: "This is one of the great Christological passages of the New Testament, declaring as it does our Lord's divine essence, pre-existence, and creative agency."[49] Thus, humanity only has power as given by God; it is not inherent to mankind in creation, since only by Christ do "all things hold together." The essence of humanity belongs to God and exists solely for the glory of God. Although Scripture makes this abundantly clear time and again, humanity, in its desire to wrestle the throne of God away from its Creator, consistently and continually resists the idea of being ruled. For the online educator, directing students to the person and work of Christ, who is the exact image of God, becomes an essential priority in student formation. Furthermore, knowing that students and faculty are often not in face-to-face proximity becomes less important to the priority of spiritual formation and conformity to the image of Christ.

Ultimately, being created in the image of God gives humanity a distinct, God-given position of dominion over the remainder of God's creation. Humanity has been placed in this position in order to point

47   O'Brien, *Colossians, Philemon*, 1982, 44:44.
48   William Hendriksen, *Galatians, Ephesians, Philippians, Colossians, and Philemon*, New Testament Commentary (Grand Rapids: Baker, 2002), 72.
49   E. K. Simpson and F. F. Bruce, *Epistles to the Ephesians and Colossians*, New International Commentary on the New Testament (Grand Rapids: Eerdmans, 1957), 192.

creation beyond humanity and to the person of Christ. Humanity is to be formed into Christ's image. Here the role of the online faculty member becomes vital. The educator must prioritize student formation over the transferring of information. However, this formation of students cannot occur if the educator has not first also been formed into the image of Christ.

A Pedagogy of Desire

Returning to Smith's argument that education should primarily be concerned not with information transfer, but rather the formation of the students, Smith presents what he calls a "pedagogy of desire." Smith emphasizes the importance of personal philosophical anthropology as the starting point for pedagogy (how and why we teach). Dismissing certain models of theological anthropology that identify mankind as either thinking or believing as reductionistic, Smith argues that mankind is at the core a desiring being, or a loving being: "To be human is to love, and it is what we love that defines who we are . . . our ultimate love is what we worship." One's ultimate desire, or worship, becomes the ultimate driving force within the life of that individual. This is true of students in both traditional and online environments.

Smith challenges the mindset that education is primarily concerned with information, and instead asserts that education should be primarily concerned with the formation of the individual. As such, education is no longer relegated to the classroom; rather, education as formation happens everywhere. Consequently, attention should be directed not just on *what* is taught, but also on *how* something is taught. This change in emphasis again puts the focus on the educator. Although Smith does not apply his research to the specific needs of the online learning environment, some natural implications exist for online course and program design. The nature of the online learning environment brings an inherent acknowledgment that education and formation are developing beyond the formal classroom.

Smith's proposed model of "The Human as Desiring Animal" starts with the recognition that humans are at their core loving beings. Second, Smith's model considers the target of an individual's love, or love's *telos*. As he indicates, what an individual or community loves defines and distinguishes that individual or community. Using the concept of "the good life" as an example, Smith explains that individuals have an ultimate desire (an affection), prior to having a cognitive idea of the good life: "Rather than being pushed by beliefs, we are pulled by a *telos* that we desire." Smith further explains that all of humanity longs for a kingdom, but not all of humanity longs for the same kingdom.

The differing longings prompt Smith's third point, which demonstrates how an individual's desires are aimed at a particular *telos*. Smith argues that one's view of the kingdom—one's longings and desires—is directed by one's dispositions (or habits). Smith understands these habits to be made (or formed) within the life of the individual, to the point where the habits become second nature. These habits are formed by one's practices or routines. This model of the human as a desiring animal has implications for educational institutions because such institutions contribute to the shaping of the routines for both the individual and community. Academic institutions direct the aim of the individual's desires. These go beyond what ideas or beliefs are being taught at an institution. Instead, they focus on the *telos* of the student's love. The faculty member becomes an important figure in shaping the student's routines and desires. These habits and routines can be fostered within both traditional and online settings.

Smith's work offers many implications for online graduate-level ministerial training. Most significant is the recognition that theological anthropology shapes and determines pedagogical practices. Additionally, based on Smith's understanding of humans as desiring beings, one should consider how the way one teaches influences a student's desires—that is, what one loves or what one worships. Smith recognizes this influence occurring beyond just the classroom. He argues that educational institutions should "also seek ways to extend and improvise upon Christian practices in order to create a learning environment that is animated by intentional practices that form the imagination and shape character."[50] Although online faculty and students are geographically separated during the educational process, the

---

50   James K. A. Smith, *Desiring the Kingdom: Worship, Worldview, and Cultural Formation* (Grand Rapids: Baker Academic, 2009), 19, 24–26, 32, 45–46, 48, 51, 53–57, 59, 73, 94, 131, 228.

student's immediate ministerial context offers opportunities for these Christian practices to be developed.

Conclusion

In conclusion, the image of God is the condition in which mankind was created. Although many understandings of the image of God have been suggested throughout scholarship, for the purposes of this project, the image of God is considered in light of its ancient Near-Eastern context. As a result of that consideration, the image of God relates to humanity's position under God (sonship) and humanity's position over creation (rulership). Sonship and rulership have implications for an individual's relationship toward God, toward others, and toward nature. However, ultimately, the true image of God is seen most clearly in the person of Jesus Christ. The goal of the Christian life is formation into the image of Christ, and as online theological training seeks to prepare students to be effective ministers of the gospel, this formation into Christ's image must be a priority.

Two specific areas related to faculty will be explored in the subsequent chapters. In the next chapter, the hiring of online faculty will be discussed. I will argue that institutions must prioritize theological competencies ahead of technological and pedagogical competencies when hiring faculty. In the subsequent chapter, faculty development and training will be considered. I will stress that the institution should prioritize the online faculty member's ongoing spiritual formation, as well as technological and pedagogical training.

Opportunities for Application

Discover

1. Analyze current curriculum to see where information transfer is prioritized over the formation of students.
2. Analyze current faculty to see how faculty members emphasize spiritual formation within their courses.

Decide

1. Determine to ground the practices of one's online courses and programs in a biblical and theological foundation.
2. Determine to emphasize formation of students into the image of Christ over merely transferring information.

Do

1. Perform a curriculum map of the institution's academic programs, giving special attention to where spiritual formation is emphasized within the curriculum.
2. Implement faculty training that emphasizes the importance of spiritual formation within courses and curriculum.

CHAPTER 6

Online Faculty and Theological Competency

Chapter 5 stressed that the goal of the Christian life is formation into the image of Christ, who is the true image of God. As online theological training seeks to prepare students to be effective ministers of the gospel, this formation into Christ's image must be prioritized above information transfer. This chapter will discuss the hiring of online faculty members, arguing that institutions must prioritize theological competencies ahead of pedagogical and technological competencies. By *prioritize* it is meant that theological anthropology provides the foundation and the alignment for both pedagogy (how and why we teach) and technology (the medium of online), meaning the order of priority is theological, then pedagogical, and then technological. Stated another way, the formation of the student into the image of Christ (theological consideration) provides the foundation for the process of teaching (pedagogical consideration), which in turn informs and shapes the way in which the online medium is utilized (technological consideration). Chapter 7 will consider online faculty development and training, emphasizing the importance of prioritizing ongoing spiritual formation amidst concerns for theological, technological, and pedagogical competencies, which is a result of considering the example of the apostle Paul's life and ministry.

The Medium of Online Education

The last chapter provided an overview of the importance of humanity's creation in the image of God, and stressed that formation into the image of Christ (the true image of God) is necessary for online ministerial training. Recognizing the unique qualities of online education, this section will build off of the foundation of one's theological understanding, and present material that explores the importance for educators to prioritize pedagogy over technology. In order to do so, a deeper look at the nature of online learning is needed. Attention is now turned to the medium of online learning.

Recognizing the Medium of Online Learning

Many mediums of communication are available for educators in both residential and online environments. Effective communication through these diverse mediums directly impacts the effectiveness of education. Speaking to the importance of medium, Marshall McLuhan explains:

> In a culture like ours, long accustomed to splitting and dividing all things as a means of control, it is sometimes a bit of a shock to be reminded that, in operational and practical fact, the medium is the message. This is merely to say that the personal and social consequences of any medium—that is, of any extension of ourselves—result from the new scale that is introduced into our affairs by each extension of ourselves, or by any new technology.[1]

Jill Schiefelbein affirms, "We do not always need a rich medium to accomplish a communication goal. A common predictor of media performance is one's ability to select the proper medium for the task at hand."[2] Similarly, Kristen Betts notes,

---

1 Marshall McLuhan, *Understanding Media* (New York: McGraw-Hill, 1964), 7.
2 Jill Schiefelbein, "Media Richness and Communication in Online Education," *Faculty Focus*, April 10, 2012, accessed November 16, 2014, http://www.facultyfocus.com/articles/online-education/media-richness-and-communication-in-online-education/.

> Interaction in face-to-face, online, and blended programs vary depending upon the channels of communication integrated into the courses. . . . Recognizing there are inherent differences between traditional and online environments, administrators and faculty must understand the importance of integrating effective communication strategies into online program development, course design, and instruction to engage, connect, and retain students.³

Educators are then to strategically select the proper medium for effective communication and education.

Differentiating between residential and online courses, Betts comments, "Even when words are not being used, communication is still taking place in a face-to-face classroom. However, in an online classroom, there is a shift and increased emphasis on words, particularly with written communication."⁴ In his study of students attending either in-person or recorded lectures, John Bassili determines that there is "no difference in learning outcomes linked to media"⁵ between students attending a lecture face-to-face, and a student watching the same lecture through video. Importantly, Bassili recognizes that the content and structure of the course likely contribute to the conclusion. The study Bassili conducted involved

> **Communication Medium**
>
> The avenue or tools through which information is shared.

> a large introductory course, and given that lectures in such courses tend to involve one-sided communication from the instructor to students, it is not surprising that information richness played a much more important role in media choice than interpersonal richness.⁶

---

3   Kristen Betts, "Lost in Translation: Importance of Effective Communication in Online Education," *Online Journal of Distance Learning Administration* 12, no. 2 (2009): 1.
4   Ibid., 10–11.
5   John N. Bassili, "Media Richness and Social Norms in the Choice to Attend Lectures or to Watch Them Online," *Journal of Educational Multimedia and Hypermedia* 17, no. 4 (2008): 471.
6   Ibid.

It is important to recognize the goal of a particular communication medium when engaging students in either an online or a residential format.[7]

Media Richness Theory is also a consideration when exploring the significance of online or residential teaching. According to Media Richness Theory, the medium chosen should correspond to the uncertainty, or the equivocality, associated within the information being communicated.[8] However, studies by Avner Caspi and Paul Gorsky concluded that "the present results failed to support this argument—there was no preference for richer media over leaner media for different types of message equivocality."[9] Morgan Shepherd and Benjamin Martz also evaluated the effectiveness of online education related to Media Richness Theory. Shepherd and Martz analyzed the media richness within various course management platforms and concluded that the

> more media used effectively in a distance program, the greater the satisfaction with that program. The effective usage of the technology (i.e., tools such as discussion forums, document sharing areas, and web casting) significantly enhances the communication and ultimately, the satisfaction with a program.[10]

---

7   Rey Hernández-Julián and Christina Peters also provide evidence that there is no significant difference between online and paper coursework. Their study consisted of two groups of Principles of Microeconomics students, one with electronic assignments and readings, and the other group with paper assignments and readings. Although the study found students who submitted their assignments online were more likely to complete the assignments, the overall grades for the course were not significantly different between the two groups. Rey Hernández-Julián and Christina Peters, "Targeting Teaching: Does the Medium Matter? Online versus Paper Coursework," *Southern Economic Journal* 78, no. 4 (2012): 1333–45, doi:10.4284/0038-4038-78.4.1333.
8   Richard L. Daft and Robert H. Lengel, "Organizational Information Requirements, Media Richness and Structural Design," *Management Science* 32, no. 5 (1986): 554–71.
9   Avner Caspi and Paul Gorsky, "Instructional Media Choice: Factors Affecting the Preferences of Distance Education Coordinators," *Journal of Educational Multimedia and Hypermedia* 14, no. 2 (2005): 187.
10 M. M. Shepherd and W. B. Martz, "Media Richness Theory and the Distance Education Environment," *Journal of Computer Information Systems* 47, no. 1 (2006): 119.

The importance of choosing the right medium, and the right techniques within that medium, are important concerns for online educators.

Neil Postman wrote much about the effects of technology (specifically television) and new media on a society. Explaining the difference between a print culture and a media culture, Postman underscores the significance to children: "All of the secrets that a print culture kept from children—about sex, violence, death and human aberration—are revealed all at once by media which do not, and cannot, exclude any audience."[11] Once created, videos and online posts are permanent fixtures within a digital society. Postman was also known for using questions as a means for evaluating the value of education in general, and more specifically of technology. Summarizing his questions, he would ask, "What is the problem to which this new technology is the answer?"[12] or "What is the tradeoff for utilizing a technology?"[13] The recognition of this tradeoff becomes important for any online educator seeking to use technology within the online medium.

Explaining the difference between a technology and a medium, Postman comments, "A technology, in other words, is merely a machine. A medium is the social and intellectual environment a machine creates."[14] It is important to keep in mind that the online medium is not the same as the face-to-face medium, and educators who do not recognize the significance of this do so at their own peril.

Neil Postman observes,

> Technology can never be the end of learning. It is, has always been, and must always be the servant of human aspiration. To regard it as our master is as degrading as it is tempting. We will

---

11 Neil Postman, "The Blurring of Childhood and the Media," *Religious Education* 82, no. 2 (1987): 294.

12 Similar questions were asked by Postman in Neil Postman, "Technology as Dazzling Distraction," *The Education Digest* 59, no. 8 (1994): 25.

13 Postman writes, "We are involved here in a tradeoff. Technology giveth and technology taketh away. . . . I am pointing out that with every advance in technology there is an inevitable and harmful side-effect." Neil Postman, "Will Our Children Only Inherit the Wind?" *Theory and Research in Social Education* 28, no. 4 (2000): 582.

14 Neil Postman, *Amusing Ourselves to Death: Public Discourse in the Age of Show Business* (New York: Penguin, 2005), 84, Kindle.

know how to employ technology in schools when we agree on the purpose of education, and not before. And we will agree on the purpose of education when we have reclaimed some great national dream which commands respect and devotion, and take hold of our children's consciousness.[15]

Continued advances in technology and continued accessibility to technology are growing factors of increased online education. These advances include access to the Internet and to computers. Related to increased access to technology is the increase of familiarity of individuals to these advances in technology. Consequently, students are becoming more comfortable communicating via advancing technology.

> **Technology**
>
> The practical application of science, specifically within this context as it relates to education at a distance.

In addition, online course design and curriculum development continue to increase. As Liu, Liao, and Pratt note, "Advances in e-learning technologies parallels a general increase in sophistication by computer users."[16] Although online education differs from residential learning, both mediums perpetually move toward one another as aspects of online education (i.e., electronic readings) are integrated into the residential classroom, and aspects of residential education (i.e., lectures and video-chat) are integrated into online courses.[17] Additionally, Sun and Cheng affirm from their study that the media richness within online education should be matched to the complexity of the information being communicated. In both measures of learning and the satisfaction level of students within the course,

> the course unit with high uncertainty and equivocality in content needs high richness media representation. On the other hand, it is ineffective to use high richness media to promote

---

15   Postman, "Will Our Children Only Inherit the Wind?" 586.
16   Su-Houn Liu, Hsiu-Li Liao, and Jean A. Pratt, "Impact of Media Richness and Flow on E-Learning Technology Acceptance," *Computers & Education* 52, no. 3 (2009): 599, doi:10.1016/j.compedu.2008.11.002.
17   For an overview of common technologies available for online course development and the Course Management Platforms (CMP) available, see Shepherd and Martz, "Media Richness Theory."

learning performance for the course unit with low uncertainty and equivocality that can be stated clearly in regular text.[18]

Recognizing the online medium for ministerial training. This brief overview of the medium of online learning has demonstrated that despite the differences of online pedagogy to the traditional classroom, the role of the faculty need not change in order to accommodate an online medium. However, recognizing these differences equips educators to utilize proper techniques to accomplish the goals of education. Learning can take place through the online medium as long as the faculty and students both select the proper communication techniques. Specific to graduate-level ministerial training, student formation can still be accomplished through the online medium, as long as the faculty, the students, and the overall institution are committed to utilizing the proper techniques for effective training.

Prioritizing Pedagogy over Technology

Simply recognizing that the medium of online learning is different from the medium of traditional face-to-face learning is not enough. Educators must learn how to effectively utilize the online medium. Research concerning the effective utilization of the medium of online education notes the importance of giving priority to pedagogy over technology, and has helped educators gain perspective on the importance of sound pedagogical principles within one's approach to teaching. These principles are often recognized as educators seek to establish the objectives of the online classroom, and as educators process through the many technologies available to them within the online teaching environment. A quick review of the literature will help establish the importance of prioritizing pedagogy over technology.

Pedagogy

The practice of teaching.

Putting pedagogy before technology. Richard Ascough stresses the need to ensure that an institution's technological advances should be "driven by sound pedagogical principles.

---

18   Pei-Chen Sun and Hsing Kenny Cheng, "The Design of Instructional Multimedia in E-Learning: A Media Richness Theory-Based Approach," *Computers & Education* 49, no. 3 (2007): 673, doi:10.1016/j.compedu.2005.11.016.

... Putting pedagogy before technology will insure quality education no matter what the content or mode of delivery."[19] He stresses that online education can be effective as long as the educator understands the medium through which the education is being processed, and he considers course design to be the most important aspect of online course delivery. He also recognizes the significance of distance education to the pedagogical environment: "If nothing else, the rise of online education has caused many of us to rethink our own pedagogical models.... Sound pedagogy is essential to the effectiveness of all of our teaching, no matter what the content or mode of delivery."[20] The objectives of the classroom and the role of the faculty within the learning environment are aspects of pedagogy that the rise of online learning has caused educators to reconsider.

Technology as a means to an end. Alan Hueth comments on the discussions surrounding online education and

> argues that the present dialogue reflects reductionist and simplistic thinking, which hinders education in both traditional face-to-face and e-learning modes.... [He combines] the pedagogical methods of Jesus Christ ... [and] reveals some important implications of this approach for both e-learning and "traditional" face-to-face instruction for CHE [Christian Higher Education] instructors and administrators.[21]

Hueth addresses what he identifies as oversimplified thinking by considering three "oversimplified, reductionist, and limiting notion[s]":

---

19 Richard S. Ascough, "Designing for Online Distance Education: Putting Pedagogy Before Technology," *Teaching Theology and Religion* 5, no. 1 (February 1, 2002): 17, doi:10.1111/1467-9647.00114. The author considers seven areas of online education: (1) "Parameters of online distance education" (17–19); (2) "Purposes of online distance education" (19–20); (3) "Planning of online courses" (20–23); (4) "Pedagogical possibilities in online distance education" (23–26); (5) "Pitfalls within online pedagogy" (26–27); (6) "Institutional faculty and student prerequisites for effective delivery of online courses" (27–28); and (7) "Predictions about the impact of online distance education" (28).
20 Ibid., 17, 20, 28.
21 Alan C. Hueth, "E-Learning and Christian Higher Education: A War of the Worlds, or Lessons in Reductionism?" *Christian Scholar's Review* 33, no. 4 (2004): 527.

(1) "close proximity guarantees learning"; (2) "learning is a simple task"; and (3) "e-learning is only about computers."[22]

Hueth provides a summary of this oversimplified thinking:

Learning is a complex and multifaceted phenomenon that Christian educators need to acknowledge and understand in a more complete way. The notion of "distance" in education is not limited to proximity. Several other distances are involved in learning, community-building, and faith-building in [Christian Higher Education]. We need to begin to view technology in a more complete way and as a means to an end.[23]

In addition, Hueth notes the significance of communication theories to education in general and online education specifically, and considers the examples provided by Jesus as the Master communicator, and also Jesus's teachings, particularly Jesus's non-verbal communications.[24]

Similar to Postman's comments, the idea of viewing technology as a means to an end is important for online graduate-level ministerial training, as the goal of spiritual formation should provide direction concerning the decisions made by educators. Viewing technology as a means to an end will allow the role of the online faculty member to be focused on the formation of students as ministers of the gospel.

Digital technology in the theological classroom. Mary Hess addresses the use of technology to enhance teaching specifically within the realm of theological education, and stresses the aspect of community within online courses.[25]

Hess argues that technology can assist a professor in six specific ways:

1. Provide a better environment for the learner
2. Provide more opportunities for students to collaborate
3. Provide teachers with a better understanding of the experiences students bring to the classroom
4. Provide accessibility to primary resources for research purposes

---

22 Ibid., 529–31.
23 Ibid., 533.
24 Ibid., 533–44.
25 Mary E. Hess, "What Difference Does It Make? Digital Technology in the Theological Classroom," *Theological Education* 41, no. 1 (January 1, 2005): 77–91.

5. Provide a mechanism to overcome time and distance limitations
6. Provide a better context for communities of faith.[26]

By utilizing the medium of online learning, the faculty member can help establish communities of students for the purpose of collaboration and faith development. In addition, the objectives of the classroom can be shaped to assist students to better achieve the goals of the course. The medium of online learning is enhanced through the development of learning communities.

Implementing online pedagogy into residential formats. Lester Ruth discusses his reconsideration of the nature of education facilitated by the conversion of a course from a residential medium into an online medium.[27] The result was a renewed approach to his teaching in both mediums. Reflecting on the impact of converting his course, and the subsequent change in his own teaching approach, the author now begins every new course preparation (online or residential) by considering how he would create a course for an online medium. One of the differences in Ruth's approach is the incorporation of discussions into his course. In designing the online course, he realized, "Discussions were not some by-product intruding into my agenda for the course. They were the course. I had to manage them well."[28]

Designing an online course forced Ruth to plan ahead and develop course schedules to fit into a module format. This encouraged him to intentionally address the entire flow of the course, rather than simply consider the next lecture. Sequencing the course became very important to him in the online format of the course.

Ruth notes that within the online medium his role as a teacher converted from the conveyer of information to the "creator of learning environments."[29] Online discussion became the focus of the course. Readings no longer prepared the student for lectures; the readings now

---

26 Ibid., 83–84.
27 Lester Ruth, "Converting My Course Converted Me: How Reinventing an On-Campus Course for an Online Environment Reinvigorated My Teaching," *Teaching Theology & Religion* 9, no. 4 (2006): 236–42, doi:10.1111/j.1467-9647.2006.00289.x.
28 Ibid., 237.
29 Ibid., 238.

prepared the students for engaging in discussions. Ultimately, Ruth says he assumed the role of a "shepherd" to the students.

Perception of the student role likewise morphed from a passive listener or reader to an active participant in the learning process. Perhaps contributing to this phenomenon, the students in an online course often differ from those in a traditional classroom, as the students in the online classroom have experience in their local church, and are actively involved in ministry. These changes in perspective generated by designing a course for the online medium also influenced Ruth's approach to pedagogy in general as he rethought the objectives of the classroom and his role as teacher.

Utilizing the online medium for ministerial training. Beyond acknowledging the differences in online learning, educators must utilize techniques and practices that lead to effective online education. These techniques and practices relate to the role of the faculty within the online course. Within graduate-level ministerial training, the goal should move beyond information transfer to the formation of students into the image of Christ (which was argued in the previous chapter), which will help develop students who can more effectively serve as ministers of the gospel within their ministry settings.

The Online Faculty Member, a Model to Follow

Having considered the need to allow pedagogy to drive the utilization of technology (through an understanding of the medium of online education), it is important to return to our consideration of the theological foundation of one's pedagogy. Since online theological education needs to focus on the formation of students into the image of Christ, it is important that faculty within the online learning environment serve as a model of spiritual formation for students. This demonstrates the institution's responsibility to prioritize a candidate's theological competencies ahead of technological and pedagogical considerations. As previously stated, by *prioritize* it is meant that theological anthropology provides the foundation and the alignment for both pedagogy (how and why we teach) and technology (the medium of online), meaning the order of priority is theological, then pedagogical, and then technological.

When searching for online faculty members, what characteristics should institutions prioritize? Primarily, the prospective faculty member should be one who can be a spiritual model in the process of student spiritual formation. Considering the need for spiritual formation within the lives of the students, the role of the online faculty member should be more than a "sage on the stage," or even "a guide on the side."[30] By *sage on a stage*, it is meant that the faculty member is seen as just the conveyer of information. By *guide on the side*, the faculty member is seen as someone who comes alongside the students and walks them through the learning process (guidance/mentorship). Information transfer and guidance are both important elements to the educational process; however, for online ministerial training, they are not enough. Information transfer or mentorship without the goal of formation falls short of the goal of ministerial training. The role of the faculty member concerns more than the transferring of information; the role of the faculty member is a formative role within the life of the student.[31] Consequently, the faculty member's role becomes "a model to follow."

> **Role of the Online Faculty Member**
>
> The role of the online faculty member is to serve as a model to follow.

Within Scripture, the need for a model to follow is evidenced within the work and ministry of the apostle Paul. He modeled what he exhorted as he established relationships with churches and taught church leaders and Christians during his ministry, even at a distance. Most explicitly, Paul's role in the spiritual formation of others is witnessed in his admonition to follow him as he follows Christ.

Paul challenges his readers to imitate his example in six Scripture passages (1 Cor 4:16; 11:1; Gal 4:12; Phil 3:17; 4:9; 2 Thess 3:7–9), and in other passages Paul offers himself as an example (see Rom 15:1–3; 1 Cor 8:13). Hawthorne, Martin, and Reid note that there

---

30 Martha Burkle and Martha Cleveland-Innes, "Defining the Role Adjustment Profile of Learners and Instructors Online," *Journal of Asynchronous Learning Networks* 17, no. 1 (n.d.): 76, accessed November 6, 2014, http://files.eric.ed.gov/fulltext/EJ1011383.pdf; Richard S. Ascough, "Designing for Online Distance Education: Putting Pedagogy before Technology," *Teaching Theology and Religion* 5, no. 1 (2002): 21, doi:10.1111/1467-9647.00114.

31 Smith, *Desiring the Kingdom*, 19, 24, 26.

are relatively few passages in the Pauline corpus where Paul uses the language of imitation . . . (1 Cor. 4:16; 11:1; Phil. 3:17; 1 Thess. 1:6; 2:14; 2 Thess. 3:6, 9). The idea of imitation, however, plays a significant . . . though sometimes misunderstood, role in Paul's ethics.[32]

Bearing in mind the importance of Paul's example of leadership, Howell lists six characteristics that Paul seeks to model for his congregations: (1) authoritative, (2) exhortational, (3) accountable, (4) affirmatory, (5) sacrificial, and (6) missional.[33] Paul lives out these characteristics in a number of ways throughout his life and ministry, including being a "pattern to imitate"[34] by living a "sacrificial" life.[35] He provides himself as a model for others to follow; he acknowledges his dependency on Christ, and his position in Christ as a "fellow servant to imitate."[36] This example of Paul is what is necessary within the life of the faculty member. It is a concern for both one's relationship to God and one's relationship to other believers.

Paul's statements concerning the need for others to follow him in different situations as he follows Christ can serve as an example for faculty in online graduate-level ministerial training. For instance, 1 Corinthians 4:16 is written within the context of a response to a prideful attitude within some of the church members at Corinth (4:6, 18–19), Galatians 4:12 is written in the context of legalism, and 2 Thessalonians 3:7–9 is written within the context of dealing with undisciplined living. The application of imitation to diverse contexts reveals the need for formation into the image of Christ in all ministry areas. Likewise, the online faculty member can model spiritual formation in many ways, and across diverse subject areas. The course content itself, the approach of the faculty member in teaching the material, and the medium through which the training occurs should all be done with Paul's example in mind. Nothing within the educational

---

32 Gerald F. Hawthorne, Ralph P. Martin, and Daniel G. Reid, eds., *Dictionary of Paul and His Letters*, First Edition (Downers Grove, IL: IVP Academic, 1993), 428.
33 Don Howell, *Servants of the Servant: A Biblical Theology of Leadership* (Eugene, OR: Wipf & Stock, 2003), 256–86.
34 Ibid., 265–66.
35 Ibid., 277–82.
36 Ibid., 266.

process falls beyond the scope of the need for formation. Even email communication, recorded lecture, video communication, and overall course design should be approached as opportunities to model Christ to students.

The nature of this imitation is important to understanding Paul's view of his role of training leaders for the church. As Hawthorne, Martin, and Reid suggest, Paul is not arrogantly desiring that the people become mirror images of himself.[37] Instead, he is merely wanting them to follow his example. The "notion of imitating some sort of moral exemplar was quite common in the ancient world."[38] But, Paul's challenge to imitate his leadership was unique in that Paul was not the focus. David Garland explains:

> This appeal was a common literary and hortatory motif in antiquity . . . but it takes a different twist in light of the divine command "Be holy, for I am holy" (Lev. 11:44–45; 19:2; 20:26; cf. Matt. 5:48) and Paul's assertion that he follows the example of Christ. He is to be followed only insofar as he adheres to the divine standard set forth by Christ.[39]

Paul viewed himself as an example for others to follow as he followed Christ, and Paul's desire was for others to be formed into the image of Christ.

Paul's desire for imitation is not the same as Jesus saying "follow me." Jesus has the rightful place of supremacy within creation, and humanity serves as a vice-regent under Christ's ultimate dominion. Thus, Paul would never put himself in the place of Christ. As Howell writes,

> Strictly speaking, Paul does not call on the churches to "follow" his leadership, for Christ alone is their leader, whereas he is a servant commissioned to enhance their allegiance to Christ. Paul sets forth himself not as a leader to follow, but as a fellow servant to imitate.[40]

---

37 Hawthorne, Martin, and Reid, *Dictionary of Paul and His Letters*, 430.
38 Ibid.
39 David E. Garland, *1 Corinthians* (Grand Rapids: Baker, 2003), 502.
40 Howell, *Servants of the Servant*, 266.

Paul understands his position in Christ and his need to model formation for others. In a similar way, the role of the online faculty member is to point students to the person and work of Christ and to further the student's formation into the image of Christ, so that students will have a proper relationship to God, to others, and to God's creation. Learning is not the ultimate goal of ministerial training; rather, formation into the image of Christ is the goal. Therefore, educators must perceive their roles as models in spiritual formation.

The example of the apostle Paul provides valuable insight for the online faculty member. Similar to the apostle Paul's role, the role of a faculty member within online graduate-level ministerial training is to strengthen, challenge, and encourage church leaders for the ultimate glory of God.

The apostle Paul's correspondence demonstrates his ability to encourage spiritual formation within the lives of church members and leaders from a distance. As it has been well established in the earlier chapters of this book, Paul's distance correspondence (i.e., letters) reinforced his physical presence with the churches.[41] Within the letters, Paul sought "to increase social presence by fostering intimacy, feelings of closeness to him by his audience."[42] Within online graduate-level ministerial training, technological and pedagogical advances provide educators unique opportunities to foster relationships with students. These relationships provide the environment for the educator to serve as a model of spiritual formation, which ultimately brings glory to God.

How does an institution ensure they have faculty who can effectively model Christ within an online course? First, the institution must prioritize theological competencies over technological and pedagogical competencies when hiring faculty. Secondly, the institution should prioritize the faculty member's ongoing spiritual formation when considering the development and evaluation of theological, technological, and pedagogical competencies.[43]

---

41 Christopher Dwight Jackson, "The Phenomenon of Social Presence in the Pauline Epistles and Its Implications for Practices of Online Education" (Ed.D. thesis, The Southern Baptist Theological Seminary, 2014), 59–62.
42 Ibid., 64.
43 Ongoing faculty development and evaluation will be the topic of chapter 7.

Hire the Right Faculty

In order to have faculty members who are models for students to follow, institutions should hire faculty who are first and foremost theologically competent. Literature concerning online Christian education is often focused on understanding the medium of online pedagogy,[44] which is an important consideration, but one that should follow from the educator's theological competency,[45] emphasizing the spiritual formation of both the faculty member and the student.

Primarily, the faculty of the Christian institution must have a commitment to a biblical worldview. This biblical worldview permeates all areas of life and determines the educator's approach to teaching and mentoring within the context of online graduate-level ministerial training. What is a worldview? It is "simply the total set of beliefs that a person has about the biggest questions in life."[46] James Sire offers a detailed explanation of a worldview:

> A worldview is a commitment, a fundamental orientation of the heart, that can be expressed as a story or in a set of presuppositions (assumptions which may be true, partially true or entirely false) that we hold (consciously or subconsciously, consistently or inconsistently) about the basic constitution of reality, and that provides the foundation on which we live and move and have our being.[47]

This worldview extends to all areas of life, but also (for the faculty member) to areas of pedagogy. The educator's engagement with students through the use of media (technology) such as video, chat, and email, should be built on the foundation of the educator's biblical worldview. In this way, the educator achieves his or her primary purpose of serving as a model.

---

[44] Dale Hale, "Online Faculty Development," in *Best Practices of Online Education*, 122, 126.

[45] Ibid., 122.

[46] Jonathan Morrow, *Think Christianly: Looking at the Intersection of Faith and Culture* (Grand Rapids: Zondervan, 2011), 69.

[47] James W. Sire, *The Universe Next Door: A Basic Worldview Catalog*, 5th ed. (Downers Grove, IL: IVP, 2009), 20.

In addition to a biblical worldview, the institution should prioritize prospective faculty members who have a proper understanding of the relationship between faith and learning. Gangel speaks to the importance of developing this integration among the faculty, and offers six principles concerning the integration of faith and learning:

1. "a commitment to the author of the Bible,"
2. "a recognition of the contemporaneity of the Bible and the Holy Spirit,"
3. "a clear understanding of the nature, source, discovery, and dissemination of truth,"
4. "designing a curriculum which is totally constructed on the centrality of special revelation,"
5. "a demand for the development of a Christian world and life view," and
6. "bibliocentric education extended to all areas of student life."[48]

In other words, all educational practices and programs and curricula should be filtered through a solid biblical-theological framework. Central to this process of integration is the faculty member who models it to the students. Gangel describes the effect of this permeation of this biblical worldview and the primacy of Scripture. He recommends a "theological sieve," which acts as a filtering system to reject information that does not correspond to a biblical worldview. Each teacher within a Christian institution must be at least an "amateur theologian," and must be able to incorporate theological and biblical teaching into his or her subject matter. This is true of both online and traditional instructors.

Conclusion

To summarize, faculty selection becomes vitally important when considering the educator's role as a model for students to follow. Just as the apostle Paul considered himself a model for others to follow, the online faculty member must also model spiritual formation. Since education is primarily about the formation of a student into the

---

[48] Kenneth O. Gangel, "Integrating Faith and Learning: Principles and Process," *Bibliotheca Sacra* 135, no. 538 (April 1, 1978): 100–105.

image of God, institutions must hire faculty who also love, desire, and model formation into the image of Christ (the true image of God). Hiring online faculty with strong theological, technological, and pedagogical competencies will ensure online graduate-level ministerial training focused on the formation of students into the image of Christ. However, the initial hiring of faculty with these competencies is not enough. Ongoing development and evaluation of online faculty members must be a priority of the institution as well. I will explore this topic in chapter 7.

Opportunities for Application

Discover

1. Analyze where one's institution has placed priority among theology, technology, and pedagogy.
2. Perform a self-assessment in order to discover if one's hiring practices in the past have considered the three areas of theology, technology, and pedagogy.

Decide

1. Determine what theological considerations are non-negotiable for one's institution.
2. Commit to hiring online faculty who can serve as a model to follow for students, and who can effectively leverage the medium of online education.

Do

1. Implement an extensive process for the hiring of online faculty, which prioritizes the theological competencies of the potential online faculty member.
2. Include in the process for hiring online faculty a means of assessing whether the faculty member will serve as a model for students to follow.

CHAPTER 7

Shaping the Spiritual Lives of Online Faculty

Not only should institutions prioritize theological competency over technological and pedagogical competency when hiring online faculty members, they should also consider the ongoing development and evaluation of online faculty. This chapter provides an overview of the theological foundation for the faculty member's ongoing role with students, and the way in which online training can serve to bring about the spiritual formation of students. This was considered in light of the apostle Paul's statement to "[b]e imitators of me, as I am of Christ" (1 Cor 11:1). As such, the previous chapter emphasized the need to hire the right faculty who can utilize technology from a distance to bring about the formation of the student.

Spiritual Formation within Online Learning

This chapter stresses that institutions must focus on the ongoing development and evaluation of online faculty and also the ongoing spiritual formation of students within courses. In other words, how can an institution ensure that the online faculty member is a model for students to follow? The information below will consider the uniqueness of the online learning environment as it relates to the formation of students.

An overview of the ability of online learning to foster spiritual formation will be presented, followed by the example of the apostle Paul as a model of ongoing spiritual formation. Whereas the previous chapter considered Paul's admonition to follow him as he followed Christ, this chapter will consider what the life and ministry of the apostle Paul looked like (which should serve as a model for faculty within online ministerial training programs). Emphasis will be placed on what true ministerial effectiveness looks like, and also the characteristic displayed by the apostle Paul.

Fostering Spiritual Formation within Online Media

It is important for educators to demonstrate that spiritual formation is taking place within courses designed for an online medium.[1] This need to demonstrate spiritual formation is directly related to one's understanding of the nature of humanity and one's understanding of how spiritual formation is accomplished. Whether through an online or residential medium of education, spiritual formation should be the central focus of students of graduate-level ministerial training. The following summaries provide an overview of the literature related to the need for spiritual formation in an online context. It is provided as evidence for both the need for spiritual formation, and also the demonstration that spiritual formation is possible (even if faculty and students are not face-to-face).

Humanity as spiritual machines or personal bodies. David Kelsey addresses distance education by considering the theological foundations of distance education:

> This essay tries to show how following that advice [the framing of the discussion on distance education in theological terms] can make a practical difference in assessing the merits of distance learning. It does so by raising questions about the theological-anthropological assumptions, respectively, or theological education and distance learning.[2]

---

[1] Association of Theological Schools, "Educational Standard," ES.4.2.3.
[2] David H. Kelsey, "Spiritual Machines, Personal Bodies, and God: Theological Education and Theological Anthropology," *Teaching Theology & Religion* 5, no. 1 (2002): 2, doi:10.1111/1467-9647.00112.

Kelsey focuses on more than just the education of clergy, including also undergraduate and graduate Christian theological education. He also notes that he is not arguing for or against distance education, but rather,

> [His] aim is to exhibit the fruitful difference it may make if analyses of proposed changes in Christian theological education are framed in explicitly doctrinal theological terms so that discussion of their merits is conducted as a discussion of what is theological about theological education.[3]

Kelsey recognizes this need for a theological foundation behind distance education and understands that this foundation affects the way in which spiritual formation is conducted within programs and courses. Kelsey offers his own suggestion for the goal of theological education: "The over-arching goal that unifies the practices making up Christian theological education is to understand God more truly."[4] This would include

> the mastery of core Christian concepts like reconciliation, grace, sin, forgiveness, love, hope, faith. . . . What theological schooling provides should be the cultivation of students' abilities to use such concepts both to articulate a vision, a synoptic view of the world and our lives in relation to God, and to discern with precision the lineaments of concrete, particular situations in people's lives in the light of faith's witness to God and God's relation to all else.[5]

The author ends the article with a question about the very nature of mankind, whether the anthropological assumptions that help keep theological education theological see students as spiritual machines or as personal bodies. The answer to the question helps to shape the educational philosophies of institutions and can potentially determine the extent to which distance education can be embraced for particular aspects of theological education.

---

3   Ibid., 3, doi:10.1111/1467-9647.00112.
4   Ibid., 6.
5   Ibid., 5.

The role of faculty in promoting spiritual formation. Roger White considers matters related to spiritual formation through distance education. The author summarizes his article by stating, "Although Christ and computer at first seem incompatible, spiritual formation can be nurtured in distance education through the creative ways in which faculty and students interact."[6] White considers Paul's letters from a distance as an indication of the ability to bring about spiritual formation from a distance.

The author also provides a list of assumptions about online teaching. These assumptions relate to the ability of educators to bring about spiritual formation among students and seek to bridge the gap between residential and online mediums of education. White makes the following suggestions: (1) Sound pedagogical methods, skills, and strategies established in traditional classrooms can translate to the online classroom; (2) motivational issues and involvement levels are important variables in online course success; and (3) a sense of community can and does occur on the Internet.[7]

The article concludes with suggestions to foster spiritual formation in distance learning classes. These suggestions include the faculty being intentional about the spiritual formation of students by stating formation as a goal of the course, the faculty member modeling vulnerability and formation to students through interaction with students, and also implementing community within the course. The role of the faculty member is seen as important to the spiritual development of students within the online medium of education.

The divine pedagogy. John Gresham addresses concerns with the format of online education and stresses the need for online education to have "deep theological justification."[8] Gresham explains the idea of the divine pedagogy is the understanding of how God teaches humanity. As mentioned in previous chapters, his work is written in response to criticism of online education, due in large part from a perceived

---

[6] Roger White, "Promoting Spiritual Formation in Distance Education," *Christian Education Journal* 3, no. 2 (2006): 303.

[7] Ibid., 310.

[8] John Gresham, "The Divine Pedagogy as a Model for Online Education," *Teaching Theology & Religion* 9, no. 1 (2006): 24, doi:10.1111/j.1467-9647.2006.00257.x.

lack of the ability of a professor to act in an incarnational manner to one's students.

By way of review on what was written earlier, Gresham roots pedagogy in the revelation of God, and ultimately in the incarnational character of Christ. He also recognizes that the church must engage culture by suggesting that the church is called to adapt its message to the circumstances of its audience according to their age, culture, and social environment. Gresham believes online education is a natural next step for education, and stresses online education attends to the needs of students where they are, and also places education in the public forum.

Gresham notes online education allows the professor to demonstrate humility. Instead of making the student come to the professor, quite literally the professor is now willing to go to the student. In this sense, the incarnational example of Christ can be evidenced within the online classroom as professors model the ability to communicate to students in an online format. Gresham suggests that the key is the instructor's communication rather than the educational environment. Gresham acknowledges that while physical presence is crucial to certain aspects of an incarnational faith, it does not seem to be an essential factor in an incarnational pedagogy.

This understanding of the professor modeling the incarnation of Christ is important for online graduate-level ministerial training. If spiritual formation is to take place within courses utilizing an online medium, the role of the faculty member must be seen as more than just facilitating learning to students. In addition, the objectives of the course must be more than just transferring information. The course must be designed to bring about the spiritual transformation of students.

Spiritual formation through the ecology of learning. Stephen Lowe and Mary Lowe argue for the possibility of spiritual formation regardless of the medium of education. The authors reflect on the nature of *spiritual development* within Association of Theological Schools (ATS) institutions and acknowledge there are diverse ways to define spiritual development. However, the authors also note that ATS schools must address the need for spiritual development of students throughout the students' program of study, irrespective of the format of education.

The authors explain the ecosystems approach as an approach that looks at the created order or at human beings (human ecology) from an ecosystems orientation and encompasses both the part and the whole. One is not sacrificed to the other because both are important for a more complete and thorough understanding of reality. They also note the importance of both individual and corporate aspects of spiritual formation. Lowe and Lowe utilize the work of Bronfenbrenner concerning spiritual formation and stress aspects of interconnectedness and reciprocity among students within educational environments.

In addition, the authors stress the larger ecosystem outside of just the theological institution. Noting the importance of social, church, and familiar aspects of one's ecosystem, the authors explain:

> We often wrongly assume that the greatest impact on a student's faith formation while in seminary is from the seminary experience. This study and the ecosystems model we are proposing would caution us against such an unfounded assumption. The seminary experience is one part of a student's larger ecosystem.[9]

The recognition of the larger ecosystem of the online student is an important consideration for educators. Spiritual formation is not limited just to the classroom, and courses designed for an online medium should take into consideration not only the past experiences that students bring to the course but also the current (and future) experiences students will have related to their ministerial training.

Online ministerial training as a necessity. Marilyn Naidoo creates a "conceptual map of the theological and pedagogical challenges for ministerial formation and highlights how the possibility of formation is being carried out in the distance-learning environment."[10] The author notes that within Africa much of the attention concerning distance education has been focused on the doing of the work rather

---

9   Stephen D. Lowe and Mary E. Lowe, "Spiritual Formation in Theological Distance Education: An Ecosystems Model," *Christian Education Journal* 7, no. 1 (January 1, 2010): 85–93.
10 Marilyn Naidoo, "Ministerial Formation of Theological Students through Distance Education," *Hervormde Teologiese Studies* 68, no. 2 (2012): 1.

than what exactly is being done and that theological education typically relates to whole person development.[11]

Although Naidoo notes both theological and sociological objections to distance education, the article concludes by recognizing a need for distance education:

> As technology advances, so does the prospect of developing and incorporating online education not only as a possibility but also a necessity. Educators can motivate growth and provide support for the personal, spiritual and ministerial growth of the student. Doing so at a distance calls for new forms and efforts.[12]

This recognition of the potential for formation within online education is important to consider. However, as the author suggests, to effectively educate at a distance the medium of online learning will need to be considered, and changes will need to be made to the way online graduate-level ministerial training is conducted.

Modeling spiritual formation from a distance. Benjamin Forrest and Mark Lamport consider the spiritual formation evidenced within Paul's correspondence with the Christians at Rome in the writing of the book of Romans: "Paul's spiritual formation of the Roman Christians offers Christian educators insight into how this process can be approached even from a distance."[13] Although not an online format of delivery, Paul's letters were a form of distance education.

Forrest and Lamport provide a summary of the literature concerning spiritual formation from a distance. In addition, they note that Paul's letter to the Christians at Rome predate his physical presence in Rome. Eight implications for spiritual formation from a distance are presented, and among the implications are the "ground for spiritual formation is the gospel" and the "location of spiritual formation is community."[14] These reflections are important for online graduate-level ministerial training, as the need for spiritual formation is

---

11 Ibid., 2.
12 Ibid., 7.
13 Benjamin K. Forrest and Mark A. Lamport, "Modeling Spiritual Formation from a Distance: Paul's Formation Transactions with the Roman Christians," *Christian Education Journal* 10, no. 1 (2013): 110.
14 Ibid., 111–17.

prioritized within ministerial training, and the development of community within online learning environments is a noted strategy for connecting students to each other and to the faculty.

Fostering spiritual formation within online learning. The need for spiritual formation within online graduate-level ministerial training is well established. This formation can take place through the efforts of the online course design, the involvement of the online faculty, or within a student's larger ecosystem; however, all of these perspectives recognize the need for spiritual development and the role the online faculty member plays within this spiritual development. Educators must understand both the medium of online learning and the nature of mankind in order to effectively focus on the development of spiritual formation through the medium of online learning. These theological, technological, and pedagogical considerations are all important for educators seeking to effectively focus the role of the faculty on the spiritual formation of online students as ministers of the gospel.

The Faculty as a Model to Follow

As the online faculty member considers himself as a model to follow, the way in which the course is taught will be greatly affected. Within online graduate-level ministerial training, the ultimate objectives of the course will move beyond simply learner-centered, or learning-centered objectives, to *formation-centered objectives*.[15] As Lois LeBar states, "If we're looking for transformation of life, we'll teach for transformation, we'll pray for transformation, and we'll not cease our efforts until we see transformation."[16]

> **Course Objectives**
>
> Course objectives should not be teacher-based, learner-based, or learning-based; rather, course objectives should be formation-based.

---

15 Thomas Esselman, "The Pedagogy of the Online Wisdom Community: Forming Church Ministers in a Digital Age," *Teaching Theology & Religion* 7, no. 3 (2004): 163, doi:10.1111/j.1467-9647.2004.00206.x; Arthur W. Bangert, "The Seven Principles of Good Practice: A Framework for Evaluating On-Line Teaching," *Internet and Higher Education* 7, no. 3 (2004): 220, 226.

16 Lois E. LeBar, *Education That Is Christian* (Colorado Springs: David C. Cook, 2000), 96.

The purpose of the M.Div. degree is theological in nature, as ATS explains; the M.Div. degree is designed "to prepare persons for ordained ministry and for general pastoral and religious leadership responsibilities in congregations and other settings."[17] The apostle Paul provides a model of spiritual formation within his writings, which builds off of the challenge to his hearers to follow his example as he follows Christ (which was explored in chapter 6). Paul sought to glorify God through the formation of individuals into the image of Christ.

Paul provides a model of spiritual formation and its importance in Philippians 2. Within this chapter, Paul models the humility of Christ in hopes that the Philippians would imitate their Lord. Hans Conzelmann builds this connection between Paul's challenge to his followers and Paul's modeling of his leadership in his comments on 1 Corinthians 11:1: "The imitation *of Christ* takes its bearings not on the person of the historical Jesus, not on his way of life, but—in the sense of Phil 2:6ff—on his saving work."[18] Richard Hays agrees that the focus of Christ was salvific in nature: "For Paul, such imitation means one thing only: shaping our lives in accordance with the pattern of Jesus' self-sacrificing love. The imitation of Christ is therefore focused on the cross."[19] Christ, as the ultimate image of God, demonstrates perfected son-ship and ruler-ship by his life and ministry. Concerning the objectives of the classroom within online graduate-level ministerial training, spiritual formation within the life of the individual is evidenced in a life that focuses on Christ and Christ's work on the cross, all for the glory of God. Online faculty members can communicate this focus in a variety of ways, including the design of the course and the course assignments, the implementation of testimonials within the course, and the faculty member's humility in interacting with online students. Emails, videos, and discussion boards are effective ways in which the online faculty member can model humility to students.

In Philippians 2, Paul offers four examples of humility to the church at Philippi by reminding them of various individuals with a

17   Association of Theological Schools, "Degree Program Standards," A.1.1.1.
18   Hans Conzelmann, *First Corinthians: A Commentary on the First Epistle to the Corinthians*, ed. George W. MacRae, S. J., trans. James W. Leitch (Philadelphia: Augsburg Fortress, 1975), 180.
19   Richard B. Hays, *First Corinthians: Interpretation: A Bible Commentary for Teaching and Preaching* (Louisville: John Knox Press, 1997), 181.

relationship to the church. Starting first with Christ (vv. 5–11), then proceeding to himself (v. 17), then Timothy (vv. 19–24), and finally Epaphroditus (vv. 25–30), Paul illustrates the way in which humility can be modeled in the lives of the believers at Philippi.[20] The ultimate example is the person of Christ, as Philippians 2:3–8 states:

> Do nothing from selfish ambition or conceit, but in humility count others more significant than yourselves. Let each of you look not only to his own interests, but also to the interests of others. Have this mind among yourselves, which is yours in Christ Jesus, who, though he was in the form of God, did not count equality with God a thing to be grasped, but emptied himself, by taking the form of a servant, being born in the likeness of men. And being found in human form, he humbled himself by becoming obedient to the point of death, even death on a cross.

The theme of humility is prevalent within the passage, and the word itself literally means "'lowliness of mind' which agrees to treat and think of others preferentially."[21] Gordon Fee notes that the idea of humility "stands in utter contradiction to the values of the Greco-Roman world, who generally considered humility not a virtue, but a shortcoming."[22] As Fee explains, true humility "has to do with a proper estimation of oneself, the stance of the creature before the Creator, utterly dependent and trusting."[23]

> **Humility**
>
> Literally meaning "lowliness of mind," humility is a proper estimation of oneself.

Although it is not the only indication of spiritual formation within the life of the Christian, humility is an essential element of the spiritual formation of the individual and demonstrates the individual's

---

20 Gerald F. Hawthorne and Ralph P. Martin, *Philippians, Revised Edition*, Revised & Expanded (Nashville: Thomas Nelson, 2004), 152.
21 Markus Bockmuehl, *The Epistle to the Philippians* (Peabody, MA: Hendrickson, 1998), 110.
22 Gordon D. Fee, *Paul's Letter to the Philippians* (Grand Rapids: Eerdmans, 1995), 188.
23 Ibid.

dependence on God for one's very existence. Forrest and Lamport provide an image of spiritual formation:

> Spiritual formation, we contend, is the process of coming to grips with our finite humanness and developing an understanding that our sufficiency lies in the person of Christ. This definition represents the "transformed mind" that Paul describes in Romans 12. The result of this type of transformation is an understanding that our position and sufficiency are wholly and completely dependent upon Christ and what he has completed for us in his death and resurrection.[24]

The online faculty member can demonstrate this understanding of one's position before Christ, and reliance on Christ, in a life of humility. Online educators' demonstrations of humility can be tracked and recorded, as much of the communication between online faculty and online students occurs through recorded videos, online discussion boards, or via email. This ability to record and review conversations and instruction is an advantage, as online administrators work to ensure online faculty members remain a model for students to follow.

Forrest and Lamport draw implications for spiritual formation from a distance from a study of Paul's correspondence with the church at Rome. They propose that spiritual formation be gospel-centered and scripturally founded.[25] In addition, they note the importance of both dialogue and the sense of community for bringing about spiritual formation within the lives of others.[26] Therefore, relationships are vital to effective spiritual formation. The authors also speak to the importance of prayer and accountability between Paul and his audience.[27]

In preparing students for full-time vocational ministry, the most important aspect of that educational experience should be a focus on the formation of that individual into the image of Christ, which will ultimately glorify God. Spiritual formation is possible from a distance when institutions and educators attend to biblical grounding, the centrality of the gospel, relationships marked by interaction, support and

---

24 Forrest and Lamport, "Modeling Spiritual Formation from a Distance," 111.
25 Ibid., 116–17.
26 Ibid., 117–18.
27 Ibid., 118–19.

accountability, and humble relationships to God, others, and creation. For educators within the field of online graduate-level ministerial training, these emphases, drawn from the example of Paul, provide a foundation from which to utilize the technological and pedagogical advances available.[28]

Ministerial Involvement of Faculty

Having reviewed some of the literature available that speaks to the ability of institutions to conduct spiritual formation from a distance, and also having considered the example of Paul and Christ as seen in Philippians 2, attention is now focused on the online student and faculty actually being involved in the work of the ministry. A commitment to preparing effective ministers, not to enacting pragmatic efficiencies, should motivate an institution offering online ministerial training programs. *Ministerial effectiveness* is not determined by such metrics as the size of the congregation, the number of programs offered at the church, the size of the church budget, or the salary of the pastor; rather, ministerial effectiveness is obedience to Christ in one's ministry.

> **Ministerial Effectiveness**
>
> Ministerial effectiveness is obedience to Christ in one's ministry.

As online students are being formed into the image of Christ through their course work, and as students interact with online faculty members who serve as models of Christian formation, the institution should make decisions that lead to the furthering of the students' obedience to Christ in all areas of the students' lives. This posture of obedience has already been considered as the picture of the humility of Christ in Philippians 2. Gordon Fee explains humility as a "proper estimation of oneself."[29] With Fee's description in view, attention is directed to the way the apostle Paul viewed himself, and his position as a son of God, and a vice-regent with God over God's creation. As a model for faculty to follow in their ongoing development and formation into the image

---

28 Specific applications based on these advances will be considered in chapter 5.
29 Fee, *Paul's Letter to the Philippians*, 188.

of Christ, attention will be given to two aspects of Paul's ministry: his testimony and his view of his position in Christ.

Paul's Testimony of Christ

Several passages of Scripture provide Paul's testimony. Acts 9 recounts his actual conversion, which is repeated by Paul in Acts 22, Acts 26, Galatians 1, and Philippians 3. Many of Paul's other writings speak of his life after the initial point of salvation. Two of the more prominent passages providing an overview of his life after conversion are found in Philippians 3:1-11 and 2 Corinthians 11:16-33.

In 1 Corinthians 15:9, Paul calls himself the least of the apostles, and in 2 Corinthians 11, he admits to enduring severe beatings with lashes and rods (vv. 24-25), to being shipwrecked (v. 25), and even needing to escape Damascus by being lowered in a basket through a window (v. 33). In 2 Corinthians 12, he speaks of a "thorn in the flesh" to "keep [him] from becoming conceited because of the surpassing greatness of the revelations" (v. 7). Although Paul speaks of his redemption throughout his writings, he is quick to boast of his weaknesses, and he remains "content with weaknesses, insults, hardships, persecutions, and calamities. For when I am weak, then I am strong" (2 Cor 12:10). It is evident from his testimony that Paul is not attempting to build himself up; rather, his focus is on "Christ crucified" (1 Cor 1:23) and glorifying God through his ministry. Paul uses his testimony to point others to Christ and not to build himself up or to promote himself.

Paul viewed his effectiveness in ministry not in the number of churches he planted nor in the number of converts he had from a message he preached; rather, Paul viewed ministerial effectiveness as obedience to Christ, no matter what the cost. When forced to boast, Paul boasts "in the Lord" (1 Cor 1:31; 2 Cor 10:17). In addition, Paul highlights his humble status in order to magnify Christ and emphasize his own position as a son of God. Paul states in Philippians 3:7-11,

> But whatever gain I had, I counted as loss for the sake of Christ. Indeed, I count everything as loss because of the surpassing worth of knowing Christ Jesus my Lord. For his sake I have suffered the loss of all things and count them as rubbish, in order that I may gain Christ and be found in him, not having a righteousness of my own that comes from the law, but that which

> comes through faith in Christ, the righteousness from God that depends on faith—that I may know him and the power of his resurrection, and may share his sufferings, becoming like him in his death, that by any means possible I may attain the resurrection from the dead.

In humility, Paul considered the testimony of what God did through his life as a picture of ministerial effectiveness. Paul's testimony is a picture of ongoing formation into the image of Christ, and Paul used his testimony as an example of a right relationship to Christ and as a picture of spiritual formation within one's life. To become more like Christ within his own life, and to assist others in doing the same, was Paul's driving focus, and likewise should be the driving purpose of online graduate-level ministerial training, and the overall purpose of faculty development and evaluation.

Ministerial effectiveness should have as an objective the testimony of the changed life (a life renewed into the image of Christ). Therefore, ministerial effectiveness (and faculty effectiveness) will relate to an individual's humble relationship to God, to others, and to God's creation, and will ultimately bring glory to God. This means that within the context of online graduate-level ministerial training, the faculty should display a commitment to ongoing ministerial effectiveness as evidence of spiritual formation. In the evaluation of online faculty, the faculty member's commitment to a local church community should be an aspect of consideration, as should the online faculty member's commitment to strengthening one's relationship to God, to others, and to God's creation.

Paul's Position in Christ

Having considered Paul's presentation of his testimony throughout his epistles, attention is now focused on another reoccurring theme throughout Paul's writing: the image of slavery. In Paul's own writings, the acknowledgment of being freed from sin is quickly followed by acknowledgment of his position in Christ as a slave of righteousness. Romans 6:18 captures this thought, noting, "And, having been set free from sin, have become slaves of righteousness." Murray Harris suggests,

> Among New Testament authors it is Paul in particular who uses slave imagery to depict the believer's relation to God or Christ. For him the Christian may be simply and aptly described as someone who serves the Lord as a slave or someone who is the Lord's slave.[30]

Paul consistently uses the imagery of slavery to identify his position in Christ, and he views this position as evidence of being formed into the image of Christ. However, Paul's use of the image of slavery does not take away from his acknowledgment of mankind's uniqueness among God's creation, or mankind's ability to have dominion as a vice-regent over God's creation. Properly understood, Paul's image of slavery speaks to mankind's son-ship (relationship to God) and ruler-ship (relationship to others).

Reflecting on Paul's use of the imagery of slavery, Ben Witherington explains that Paul "turns the tables on the strong by calling for them to imitate him in his slavish behavior, which turns conventional rules and expectations upside down."[31] Witherington's comments are made in the context of 1 Corinthians 8–10. Specifically considering chapter 9, it becomes apparent that Paul desires to emphasize his lowly status:

> For though I am free from all, I have made myself a servant [slave] to all, that I might win more of them. To the Jews I became as a Jew, in order to win Jews. To those under the law I became as one under the law (though not being myself under the law) that I might win those under the law. To those outside the law I became as one outside the law (not being outside the law of God but under the law of Christ) that I might win those outside the law. To the weak I became weak, that I might win the weak. I have become all things to all people, that by all means I might save some. I do it all for the sake of the gospel, that I may share with them in its blessings. (2 Cor 9:19–23)

---

30   Murray J. Harris, *Slave of Christ: A New Testament Metaphor for Total Devotion to Christ* (Downers Grove, IL: IVP Academic, 2001), 154.
31   Ben Witherington, *Conflict and Community in Corinth: A Socio-Rhetorical Commentary on 1 and 2 Corinthians* (Grand Rapids: Eerdmans, 1995), 229.

Paul considers his ministerial effectiveness to be directly tied to his position in Christ, and all of his training is for the "sake of the gospel," which will bring glory to God.

The Greek word for slave in 1 Corinthians 9:19 means "to make a slave." Paul uses this idea of himself throughout many of his books, noting his position as a slave of Christ. Paul also uses this word to describe Christ in Philippians 2:7. When believers understand their relationship to God, they demonstrate humility by ceasing to strive to be the Lord of their own lives. John MacArthur explains: "We no longer live for ourselves."[32] The apostle Paul models this understanding throughout his ministry and seeks to help others model this understanding as well as to interact with God, with others, and with God's creation. Within online graduate-level ministerial training, the development and evaluation of the faculty should ultimately be focused on the formation of students into effective ministers of the gospel, which will be evidenced by the individual's testimony as being redeemed, and as being a slave to righteousness (Romans 6). The online faculty member can demonstrate this understanding by acting in humility toward online students and by demonstrating a proper relationship to God, to others, and to God's creation by service to others and commitment to the local community of believers.

Paul understands that his ministry is really not his ministry at all; it is the ministry of Jesus Christ through Paul, for the glory of God. Harris suggests, "Freedom from slavery is followed by freedom in slavery."[33] Craig Blomberg summarizes both Paul's testimony and Paul's challenge to his followers to imitate his leadership:

> It is as if Paul is saying, "Do you want to know what it means to live a consistent Christian life, properly balancing freedom and restraint? Then watch me, follow me, and live with me. I may not be perfect, but I try to imitate the selfless life Christ lived, and to the extent that I succeed, you should do the same."[34]

---

[32] John MacArthur, *Slave: The Hidden Truth about Your Identity in Christ* (Nashville: Thomas Nelson, 2010), 200–209. MacArthur notes four paradoxes related to the believer's position as a slave of Christ: (1) slavery brings freedom, (2) slavery ends prejudice, (3) slavery magnifies grace, and (4) slavery pictures salvation.

[33] Harris, *Slave of Christ*, 154.

[34] Craig L. Blomberg, *First Corinthians*, The NIV Application Commentary (Grand Rapids: Zondervan, 1994), 205.

Paul's desire to testify to the person and work of Christ becomes a model for others to follow and an example of what spiritual formation looks like within the life of the individual. Modeling Christ becomes the focus of the Christian life, which affects the way in which a minister views oneself, and the way in which the minister views those being ministered to through their ministry. Consequently, one's relationships to God, to others, and to God's creation are all affected. Within online graduate-level ministerial training, the development and evaluation of the online faculty member should focus on preparing individuals to be effective ministers of the gospel, by demonstrating the redemption of Christ within one's life, and by demonstrating the posture of humility through the acknowledgment of one's slavery to Christ.

Modeling Christ

Within the context of online graduate-level ministerial training, faculty and students find themselves in an interesting situation. On the one hand, online faculty members lead students with a focus on the spiritual formation of students into the image of Christ. On the other hand, online students are being prepared to lead others within the context of the local church, which means students are being prepared to be leaders of others. As such, it is important to consider what this leadership looks like specific to spiritual formation, for the online faculty member (who is a model to follow), the online student (who is being formed into the image of Christ), and also for the individuals who will be ministered to by the students.

Paul's statements about humility and modeling Christ are written within the context of Paul leading others, and Paul utilizes his position in Christ to help him be a more effective leader of God's people. Implications of Paul's example for the purpose of online graduate-level ministerial training are numerous, as M.Div. programs are designed to train graduates for ministerial effectiveness. In the following section, four specific areas are mentioned and explained, all of which help to ensure the ongoing development and evaluation of the online faculty members so that they are a model to follow. Formation into the image of Christ should lead online faculty and students to demonstrate Christlike characteristics, which include being a person of character, demonstrating a willingness to suffer, exhibiting strength with humility, and leading through serving. These factors should be evidenced within online faculty not only throughout the hiring process, but also through the ongoing evaluation and development of the online faculty member.

A Person of Character

First, formation into the image of Christ means the individual is a person of character. Don Howell speaks to the character of a leader by listing three important components of the servant leader—character, motive, and agenda. Although it is acknowledged that "character is not essential to leadership,"[35] as there are many examples of leaders without Christlike character throughout history who could gather and organize others, it should also be noted that "character is what makes a leader worth following."[36] Howell explains:

> Who the leader is and is becoming in one's essential being (character), why the leader undertakes a course of action (motive), and what the leader pursues as the defined mission (agenda) are, we believe, the core constituents and interrelated foci of the kind of leadership enjoined in Holy Scripture.[37]

The character of the online faculty member is vitally important to both the institution and to the students who sit under his teachings. Just as the image of God affects all aspects of humanity and points to humanity's uniqueness among God's creation, the individual's character permeates all of his life. Online faculty who model character within their own lives will be more prepared to help form online students who also model character. The demonstration of character can be evidenced within the communication between online faculty and students and between online faculty and administrators of the university. Being a person of character means that the online faculty member will fulfill the job he or she is being paid to do, such as effectively interacting with

---

[35] Andy Stanley, *Next Generation Leader: 5 Essentials for Those Who Will Shape the Future* (Sisters, OR: Multnomah, 2006), 131.
[36] Ibid.
[37] Howell, *Servants of the Servant*, 296.

students, timeliness in grading assignments, timeliness in responding to students via email and discussion boards, and living a life that can be followed by students.

Willingness to Suffer

A second consideration concerning formation into the image of Christ is the willingness of the individual to suffer for the sake of Christ. The context of the discussion in Philippians 2 is the last paragraph of Philippians 1 (vv. 27–30), which speaks to the suffering (v. 29) endured by the Christians at Philippi. Commenting on 1 Corinthians 10:23–11:1, Fee writes,

> For Paul it is a question of love and freedom. . . . Knowledge and rights lead to pride; they are ultimately non-Christian because the bottom line is selfishness—freedom to do as I please when I please. Love and freedom lead to edification; they are ultimately Christian because the bottom line is the benefit of someone else—that they may be saved (v. 33).[38]

The mindset of humility should be evidenced in one's understanding of the role of suffering. Although Christ is the "image of the invisible God" (Col 1:15), and has ultimate dominion over all of creation (Col 1:16), Hebrews 5:8 explains that Christ "learned obedience through what he suffered." Likewise, the apostle Paul provides an example for others to follow not only in what he suffered, but also in his response to that suffering. Through Paul's use of slave imagery, he shows that the Christian life is a life of "living sacrifice" (Rom 12:1) to God. This willingness to suffer is modeled by Christ and by the apostle Paul, and provides educators within online graduate-level ministerial training the perspective necessary to effectively train students to be effective ministers of the gospel. Evidence of suffering is often seen in the online faculty member's involvement within the context of local church ministry. These examples for online students become models of effective and obedient ministry on behalf of the online faculty member.

---

[38] Gordon D. Fee, *The First Epistle to the Corinthians* (Grand Rapids: Eerdmans, 1987), 477–78.

Strength with Humility

A third consideration concerning formation into the image of Christ relates to the humility of the individual. The humility demonstrated by the apostle Paul has already been considered; however, Paul's posture of humility does not indicate weakness. Reflecting on the ministry of the apostle Paul, Howell states, "Paul is not afraid to directly confront individuals or groups of individuals who seek to undermine the apostolic foundation of the churches,"[39] which speaks to Paul's relationship with the individuals within the churches. In commenting on the context of 1 Corinthians 4:14–21, Don Carson notes, "And where deviations from the way of the cross are sufficiently notorious, that leader may have to resort to some form of discipline."[40] The apostle Paul even states in 2 Corinthians 12:10, "For the sake of Christ, then, I am content with weaknesses, insults, hardships, persecutions, and calamities. For when I am weak, then I am strong." Throughout his ministry, Paul consistently modeled strength with humility, an approach that affected his relationships to God, to others, and to God's creation.

Howell also comments on the manner in which Paul carried out his ministry:

> Though Paul is an authoritative leader, he is not authoritarian, demanding compliance to satisfy a psychological need to lord it over others. He is respectful, gracious and non-coercive, never controlling, manipulative or threatening. Paul is deeply conscious that the apostolic authority delegated to him is for building up the churches, never for tearing them down (2 Cor 10:8; 13:10).[41]

This attitude can only be displayed when the online faculty member is in a right relationship with Christ and when the faculty member understands the significance of the model set for followers.

The apostle Paul understood this principle and challenges believers today to model his leadership, not so he would be exalted, but "so that at the name of Jesus every knee should bow, in heaven and on earth and under the earth, and every tongue confess that Jesus Christ is

---

39 Howell, *Servants of the Servant*, 257.
40 D. A. Carson, *The Cross and Christian Ministry: Leadership Lessons from 1 Corinthians* (Grand Rapids: Baker, 2004), loc. 1250, Kindle.
41 Howell, *Servants of the Servant*, 260.

Lord, to the glory of God the Father" (Phil 2:10–11). He challenges his followers to model his leadership, as long as he is following Christ, and he provides many opportunities for his followers to see his leadership in action. Most notably, Paul follows the modeling of Christ by humbly obeying the commands of Jesus so that Jesus may be glorified and that the gospel message may be proclaimed. In a similar way, faculty within the setting of online graduate-level ministerial training can model strength with humility for students, and they can educate students to model strength with humility throughout the students' ministry. Faculty members can be fair with their grading standards, consistent in the application of policies within the online course, and non-threatening in their interaction with students.

Leading through Serving

Finally, formation into the image of Christ means that the online faculty member and the online student will lead others through serving others. Peter Northouse explains the concept of servant leadership as a paradox that requires the leader to consider the follower first.[42] Northouse also notes servant leadership emphasizes the belief that leaders should be altruistic and humanist, using the leader's position to empower and enable others.[43] This attitude of a servant leader is evidenced within the life and ministry of the apostle Paul and can serve as a model for online faculty and students. This paradox is also seen in the example of Christ as ruler over all of creation, and also the humble servant of God (Philippians 2). Paul's willingness to "become all things to all people" (1 Cor 9:22) for the sake of the gospel is an example of this servant mindset. In addition, Paul's continued use of slave imagery to describe his own life is further evidence of his view of servant leadership.

Among the most influential theorists on servant leadership is Robert Greenleaf, who explains, "The great leader is seen as servant first."[44] Larry Spears continued Greenleaf's work and identified ten

---

42 Peter G. Northouse, *Leadership: Theory and Practice*, 6th ed. (Los Angeles: Sage, 2013), 219.
43 Ibid., 233.
44 Robert K. Greenleaf, *Servant Leadership: A Journey into the Nature of Legitimate Power and Greatness*, ed. Larry C. Spears, 25th anniversary ed. (New York: Paulist, 2002), 21.

characteristics as central to servant leaders: listening, empathy, healing, awareness, persuasion, conceptualization, foresight, stewardship, commitment to growth of people, and building community.[45] However, more than just a set of characteristics, servant leadership is a philosophy and set of behaviors.[46] For the online faculty member, servant leadership through one's courses and interaction with students must become a way of life, as the image of God affects all areas of life, including relationships to God, to others, and to God's creation. Timothy Laniak explains that "biblically speaking, a human leader is none other than God leading his own people through an anointed servant."[47] The online faculty member must keep the formation of students into the image of Christ a priority within online graduate-level ministerial training and seek to model this formation within his or her own life so that God will ultimately be glorified. Replying to an email in a timely manner, re-explaining assignment instructions, and making an extra phone call to reach out to an online student are all ways in which the online faculty member can demonstrate leadership through one's service to students.

Develop and Evaluate Faculty

In order to ensure online faculty members are a model for students to follow, institutions must develop and evaluate the online faculty according to theological considerations. Standards related to just technological and pedagogical competency are not enough, because the role of the online faculty member extends beyond efficiently managing an online classroom. The faculty member should model spiritual formation into the image of Christ. Thus, faculty development and evaluation should focus on spiritual development and evaluation.

The example of Paul is helpful. Institutions should seek to develop faculty into persons of character, who demonstrate a willingness to

---

45 Larry Spears, "The Understanding and Practice of Servant-Leadership," School of Leadership Studies: Regent University, August 2005, 3–4, accessed January 21, 2015, https://www.regent.edu/acad/global/publications/sl_proceedings/2005/spears_practice.pdf.
46 Northouse, *Leadership*, 236.
47 Timothy Laniak, *Shepherds after My Own Heart: Pastoral Traditions and Leadership in the Bible* (Downers Grove, IL: IVP, 2006), 92.

suffer, who exhibit strength with humility, and who lead through serving. As Pazmiño argues, "The five Christian virtues of truth, love, faith, hope, and joy [should] serve to guide teaching that faithfully represents Jesus today."[48] In other words, teachers should demonstrate the love of Christ throughout their teaching, which is a sign of the teacher's integrity.[49] The need for the foundation of a biblical view of human nature is seen in Pazmiño's statements about the image of God:

> Persons are created in the very image of God (Gen. 1:27) and as God's creatures are accountable to fulfill God's purposes for all of creation. Persons find their primary identity as children of God and potentially friends and followers of Jesus Christ and vessels of the Holy Spirit in the world.[50]

In addition, Pazmiño stresses the teacher should have a love for teaching and for the students.[51] This foundation of love and commitment to others is a direct result of humanity's creation in the image of God and is an essential characteristic of faculty development and evaluation. When this theological framework is lacking, the emphasis of development tends to focus on technological competency, and not formation into the image of Christ.[52] Instead, the online faculty member should be developed and evaluated based on the image of Christ.

Faculty should also harbor the Christian virtues of faith, hope, and joy. Explaining the significance of faith, Pazmiño states, "The venture of Christian teaching calls for faith in one's own identity as a teacher and faith in the presence of God's Spirit to empower the effort."[53] The aspect of hope in teaching in Jesus's name "fosters a sense of hope for persons, families, groups, and communities."[54] The author also explains the joy that comes from teaching: "I would maintain that joy is the emotion closest to the heart of God and that our human celebration of

---

48 Robert W. Pazmiño, "Teaching in the Name of Jesus," *Christian Education Journal* 5, no. 1 (2008): 171.
49 Ibid., 175.
50 Ibid., 173.
51 Ibid., 176–79.
52 For an example, see Jason Baker, "Characteristics of Successful Online Students," in *Best Practices of Online Education*, 103–5.
53 Pazmiño, "Teaching in the Name of Jesus," 179.
54 Ibid., 181.

joy in both public worship and festival or fiesta provides the occasion for our hearts to touch or be in communion with God's heart."[55] Within the context of online graduate-level ministerial training, joy can be displayed through communication with students regarding course content and by connecting them with local church gatherings. The virtues of Christ as displayed through the faculty member are an indication of the formation of that faculty member into the image of Christ. To that end, institutions must encourage these standards through faculty development and evaluation.

Opportunities for Application

Discover

1. Analyze the areas of theology, technology, and pedagogy to see where one's institutions may have areas of weakness.
2. Survey faculty to see if they are actively involved in ministry.

Decide

1. Determine to make sure the success of an online course is measured by more than just information transfer.
2. Choose a set of theological standards, or competencies, regarding which faculty will be regularly evaluated—competencies that will help to demonstrate ongoing spiritual formation in the faculty member.

Do

1. Implement ongoing professional development for online faculty that provides training in the three specific areas of theology, technology, and pedagogy.
2. Provide a system of accountability for online faculty by instituting a leadership structure within the online program that includes mentors for online faculty members.

---

[55] Ibid., 186.

Section III
Better Practices in the Classroom

How Ministry Context Provides a Framework for Effective Online Learning

John Cartwright

A casual scan of the educational landscape indicates that nearly all educational institutions have embraced online learning in recent years, and Christian universities and theological seminaries are no exception. A recent study by the Babson Survey Research and Quahog Research Group stated that the number of students taking an online course grew by 570,000 in 2012 to 6.7 million.[1] Among these 6.7 million students are some noteworthy demographics: 67 percent are female, 85 percent are over twenty-four, and 30 percent are enrolled in graduate programs.[2]

Despite growth in online learning even among theological institutions, the decision to offer online programs has not always been rooted in deep pedagogical or theological reflection. Schools, even theological schools, compete for a share of the growing market of students that see online learning as a viable option to meet their educational goals. However, in this quest, has serious thought been given to the

---

1. I. Elaine Allen and Jeff Seaman, "Changing Course: Ten Years of Tracking Online Education in the United States," 4, accessed January 9, 2013, http://www.onlinelearningsurvey.com/reports/changingcourse.pdf.
2. Noel-Levitz, "2011 Research Report: National Online Learners Priorities Report," 5, accessed January 9, 2013, https://www.noellevitz.com/upload/Papers_and_Research/2011/PSOL_report%202011.pdf. The conventional age range for college students is eighteen to twenty-four.

uniqueness of the online learning environment (or the online learner) and the potential impact of that unique character on how ministry training is accomplished? Schools with residential programs may often simply repackage these degree programs to be offered on the Internet rather than in the classroom, changing only what must be changed in order to allow students to take the class online instead of in person.

Online programs are growing for a variety of reasons. Many individuals are able to access undergraduate and graduate programs of study that were simply inaccessible before. The inability to access an education may be due to life circumstances, such as full-time employment that does not allow for attendance in class or not being geographically located near an educational institution that offers the desired program. Convenience, flexible pacing, and work schedule rank highly as factors leading to enrollment in online programs.[3] These programs allow students to pursue educational goals without quitting their jobs or moving. Those benefits can be a tremendous advantage—for example, when ministers who desire to complete a seminary degree no longer have to resign, uproot their families, and leave their faith communities in order to go back to school. Theological institutions, therefore, must consciously decide as to whether or not they will offer online programs. Accredited schools that have yet to offer online programs, or at least online courses, are most likely in the minority. Some schools may only offer degree programs that are partially online. On the other hand, other institutions that offer theological training have chosen to offer fully online degree programs.

Much has been written regarding the best practices for online education.[4] A number of formative and foundational works exist that

---

3   Ibid.
4   Arthur W. Bangert, "The Seven Principles of Good Practice: A Framework for Evaluating On-Line Teaching," *Internet and Higher Education* 7, no. 3 (2004): 217–32; Arthur W. Chickering and Zelda F Gamson, "Seven Principles for Good Practice in Undergraduate Education," *Biochemical Education* 17, no. 3 (1989): 140–41; Charles Graham et al., "Seven Principles of Effective Teaching: A Practical Lens for Evaluating Online Courses," *Technology Source* (January 2001), accessed September 19, 2013, http://eric.ed.gov/?id=EJ629854; Morris Keeton, "Best Online Instructional Practices: Report of Phase I of an Ongoing Study | The Sloan Consortium," *The Journal of Asynchronous Learning Networks* 8, no. 2 (2004): 75–100; Mark A. Maddix, James R. Estep, and Mary E. Lowe, *Best Practices of Online Education: A Guide*

are used by accrediting agencies in order to evaluate the effectiveness of online learning programs. Several articles, some of which are written from the perspective of theological education, have attempted to answer the question, "What are the best practices for online education?"[5] Others focus on tackling potential problems created by the distance of online education.[6] Some literature is available that deals with assessment of online programs.[7] Finally, much of this book, thus far, has analyzed the theological aspects of online education. But how much consideration has been given to the pedagogical differences found in the online learning environment, especially in online theological programs?

This section of the book will offer a framework of best practices for online theological ministry programs. The goal here is to harmonize the ideas related to the best pedagogical and theological practices. The discussion begins with a review of the already-established general

for Christian Higher Education (Charlotte, NC: Information Age, 2012); Michael G. Moore and William G. Anderson, *Handbook of Distance Education* (Mahwah, NJ: Erlbaum, 2003); Joan Thormann, *The Complete Step-by-Step Guide to Designing and Teaching Online Courses* (New York: Teachers College Press, 2012); Marjorie Vai, *Essentials of Online Course Design: A Standards-Based Guide* (New York: Routledge, 2011); Nichole Vasser, "Instructional Design Processes and Traditional Colleges," *Online Journal of Distance Learning Administration* 13, no. 4 (December 15, 2010), accessed September 24, 2013, http://www.westga.edu/~distance/ojdla/winter134/vasser134.html; Southern Association of Colleges and Schools Commission on Colleges, "Best Practices for Electronically Offered Degree and Certificate Programs," accessed September 19, 2013, www.sacscoc.org/pdf/commadap.pdf.

5   Stephen Paul Raybon, "An Evaluation of Best Practices in Online Continuing Theological Education" (Ed.D. diss., University of North Carolina at Charlotte, 2012); Arthur Chickering and Zelda Gamson, "Implementing the Seven Principles of Good Practice in Undergraduate Education: Technology as Lever," *Accounting Education News* (Spring 2001): 9–10; Howell and Baker, "Good (Best) Practices"; Sorel Reisman, John Flores, and Denzil Edge, *Electronic Learning Communities: Current Issues and Best Practices* (Greenwich, CT: Information Age, 2003); Glen C. J. Byer et al., "Generative Neo-Cyberculture in the Modern Seminary," *Teaching Theology & Religion* 5, no. 2 (2002): 113–17.

6   E. C. Boling et al., "Cutting the Distance in Distance Education: Perspectives on What Promotes Positive, Online Learning Experiences," *The Internet and Higher Education* 15, no. 2 (March 2012): 118–26.

7   Qi Wang, "Quality Assurance-Best Practices for Assessing Online Programs," *International Journal on ELearning* 5, no. 2 (2006): 265–74.

best practices for online education.⁸ Indeed, "best practices" are "best practices" regardless of the subject matter. After establishing these general best practices of online education, a description will be given of recent research among experts regarding best practices in the area of online ministry training. Finally, the idea of utilizing an online student's in-context ministry setting will be explored as, perhaps, the single greatest advantage over the bricks-and-mortar setting.

---

8   This starting place is really a discussion that builds on what has already been established throughout this work.

CHAPTER 8

Best Practices for Online Learning

Online education involves at least two unique features that require special consideration for educational institutions. The first and most obvious of these unique features is the "online" element itself—that is, the technological learning platform. When learning moves from a traditional bricks-and-mortar classroom to the Internet, the entire mode of instruction changes. Online learning represents a transition of education as a lecture-driven environment to a learning experience that is highly self-directed. In an online learning environment, the potential of theological education being content-rich, but poor in the areas of educational and developmental theory, is very real.

Bricks-and-mortar

Bricks-and-mortar education is a colloquial reference to learning that takes place in a residential face-to-face environment.

A second unique feature of online education is the demographic of the average online student. As mentioned earlier, the online student is generally older than the residential student—a fact also true of graduate students. A significant literature base exists regarding adult learning theory. Additionally, one can make a strong case, based on the demographics of online students, for online learning to take an approach that better accounts for the ways adults learn.[1] Students are choosing online learning for reasons of flexibility and convenience. Although these factors should not be the sole reason that an institution offers online education, schools should not ignore them either. Rather, they are factors that should be at least considered when designing degree programs and coursework. Of course, the danger in this is that programs can fall prey to pure pragmatism, while the objectives of a ministry degree program are compromised. In order to discuss the general best practices for online learning, this chapter will explore statistics related to the typical online learner, as well as adult learning theory and its relationship to online learning. Once the general best practices are explored, the discussion can move to the more narrow application of theological ministry training.

The Online Student

The Online Learning Consortium (formally The Sloan Consortium) "is the leading professional online learning society devoted to advancing quality e-Education learning into the mainstream of education through its community."[2] Since 1992, this non-profit has been "fueling the development of online learning in American higher education."[3] One of the strengths of the Online Learning Consortium is its research. From the *Journal of Asynchronous Learning Networks* to its Survey Reports, this organization is a leader in producing key research on the subject of online learning.[4] In 2003, the consortium produced

---

[1] Kathleen Yoshino Gustafson, "Assessment of Self-Directed Learning in an Online Context in the Community College Setting" (Ed.D. diss., University of California, San Diego and California State University, San Marcos, 2010). Tzipora Katz, "Adult Online Learning: A Study of Attitude, Motivation, and Engagement" (Ph.D. diss., Capella University, 2010); Rosemary Han Kim, "Self-Directed Learning Management System: Enabling Competency and Self-Efficacy in Online Learning Environments" (Ph.D. diss., Claremont Graduate University, 2010).
[2] The Sloan Consortium, "About Sloan-C," accessed September 24, 2013, http://sloanconsortium.org/aboutus.
[3] Ibid.
[4] The Sloan Consortium, "Research and Publications," accessed September 24, 2013, http://sloanconsortium.org/sloanc_publications.

its first comprehensive look at online education in the United States.[5] In the fall of 2002, research showed that 1.6 million students took at least one online course. This represented about 2.6 percent of all enrolled students.[6] Since this initial report, the Online Learning Consortium has produced similar annual reports.[7] The most recent release gives comprehensive data for the past ten years of online education. Despite the fact that overall enrollment in residential higher education declined in 2011 by 0.1 (or 22,013 students), the number of students taking at least one online course grew by over 570,000.[8] Since the fall of 2002, the number of students taking at least one online course has grown from 1.6 million (9.6 percent of all enrolled students) to more than 6.7 million (32 percent of all enrolled students) in the fall of 2011. Even in 2002, when the Online Learning Consortium first began its research, 28.3 percent of higher education institutions had no online offerings. In the most recent research, that number is down to 13.5 percent.[9] Additionally, the percentage of schools offering complete online programs has grown from 34.5 percent to 62.4 percent.[10]

5   I. Elaine Allen and Jeff Seaman, *Entering the Mainstream: The Quality and Extent of Online Education in the United States, 2003 and 2004* (Needham, MA: Babson Survey Research Group, 2004).
6   Ibid., 17–19.
7   I. Elaine Allen and Jeff Seaman, *Sizing the Opportunity: The Quality and Extent of Online Education in the United States, 2002 and 2003* (Needham, MA: Babson Survey Research Group, 2003); Allen and Seaman, *Entering the Mainstream*; idem, *Growing by Degrees: Online Education in the United States, 2005* (Needham, MA: Babson Survey Research Group, 2005); idem, *Making the Grade Cover Making the Grade: Online Education in the United States, 2006* (Needham, MA: Babson Survey Research Group, 2006); idem, *Online Nation: Five Years of Growth in Online Learning | The Sloan Consortium* (Needham, MA: Babson Survey Research Group, 2007); idem, *Staying the Course: Online Education in the United States, 2008 | The Sloan Consortium* (Needham, MA: Babson Survey Research Group, 2008); idem, *Learning on Demand: Online Education in the United States, 2009 | The Sloan Consortium* (Needham, MA: Babson Survey Research Group, 2009); idem, *Class Differences: Online Education in the United States, 2010* (Needham, MA: Babson Survey Research Group, 2010); idem, *Going the Distance: Online Education in the United States, 2011* (Needham, MA: Babson Survey Research Group, 2011); idem, *Changing Course: Ten Years of Tracking Online Education in the United States* (Needham, MA: Babson Survey Research Group, 2013).
8   Allen and Seaman, *Changing Course*, 17.
9   Ibid., 20.
10 Ibid.

All of this demonstrates that online learning is growing and will continue to grow, making research in the area of best practices that much more important. Once one considers the growth rate of online learning compared to its traditional counterpart, the case for the research becomes even clearer.

Why are these nearly seven million students enrolled in online learning? The Noel-Levitz National Online Learners Priorities Report gives some helpful information in answering this question. The three highest enrollment factors for online students, in order of importance, are convenience, flexible pacing for completing a program, and work schedule. These factors are typical for adult learners, as was discussed earlier in this chapter. The sheer number of students choosing to pursue their degrees online makes the identification of best practices in online theological ministry training an urgent matter.

Online Practices and Adult Learning Theory

When considering the broad category for best practices in online learning, at least three questions need to be answered. First, what impact should the general characteristics of the online learner have on the development of best practices for online learning? Second, what are the identifiable best practices for online learning? Third, how do policies and regulations in the area of accreditation fit into best practices? In one sense, accreditation policies are also considered best practices in that they are important enough to be required by accrediting agencies. In another sense, they should be viewed as a baseline, in that they do not address more pedagogically relevant concerns.

So to answer the first question, what impact should knowledge of the online learner have on the development of best practices for online learning? The average age of the undergraduate online learner is thirty-four.[11] If this is the case, then most likely the average age of the graduate online learner is also older than typical graduate students.

---

11   Classes and Careers, "Student Demographics," accessed January 10, 2013, http://www.classesandcareers.com/education/infographics/student-demographics-infographic/.

Since the 1920s, the question of how adults learn has been a focus of scholars.[12] Eventually, "andragogy" became the term people used to describe how adults learn. Malcolm Knowles describes the arrival at this term as something that he picked up from European adult educators and then coined in an article in the mid-1960s.[13]

> **Andragogy**
>
> Term used to describe the study and practice of how adults learn.

Several works of Knowles speak extensively to his study on the topic of andragogy.[14] Merriam gives five assumptions that underlie andragogy—all of which are relevant to the best practices of online learning:

> The five assumptions underlying andragogy describe the adult learner as someone who (1) has an independent self-concept and who can direct his or her own learning, (2) has accumulated a reservoir of life experiences that is a rich resource for learning, (3) has learning needs closely related to changing social roles, (4) is problem-centered and interested in immediate application of knowledge, and (5) is motivated to learn by internal rather than external factors.[15]

Given what is known of the average age of the online learner, this should directly impact the best practices for online learning, and it has.[16] With an understanding of the typical online learner, and based

---

12   Sharan B. Merriam, "Andragogy and Self-Directed Learning: Pillars of Adult Learning Theory," *New Directions for Adult and Continuing Education* 2001, no. 89 (2001): 3.
13   Malcolm Shepherd Knowles, *The Modern Practice of Adult Education: From Pedagogy to Andragogy*, rev. and updated ed. (Englewood Cliffs, NJ: Cambridge Adult Education, 1980), 42.
14   Malcolm Shepherd Knowles, *Self-Directed Learning: A Guide for Learners and Teachers* (Chicago: Association Press, 1975); Malcolm S. Knowles, *The Adult Learner: The Definitive Classic in Adult Education and Human Resource Development*, 6th ed. (Amsterdam: Elsevier, 2005); Malcolm Shepherd Knowles, *The Modern Practice of Adult Education: Andragogy in Action*, The Jossey-Bass Management Series (San Francisco: Jossey-Bass, 1984).
15   Merriam, "Andragogy and Self-Directed Learning," 5.
16   D. Billington, "Seven Characteristics of Highly Effective Adult Learning Programs," *New Horizons for Learning*, 1996, accessed January 1, 2013, http://www.newhorizons.org/lifelong/workplace/billington.htm; Ralph Brockett,

on existing adult learning theory, Frey and Alman offer ten extensive recommendations for those who develop and teach online courses:

1. State clear expectations:
   - Provide detailed syllabus with schedule, grading criteria, assignments, number of postings per week, deadlines, office hours.
   - Avoid changing aspects of the course once it begins.
   - State contingency plans for when the technology fails.

2. Incorporate multiple forms of feedback into course:
   - Use specific, consistent feedback from both learners and instructor.
   - Grade assignments with specific, stated criteria.
   - Provide both general and specific feedback to individuals, teams, and the whole class.

3. Provide regular communication to individual learners and the group:
   - Respond to email within twenty-four hours.
   - Personalize the class setting.

"Is It Time to Move On? Reflections on a Research Agenda for Self-Directed Learning in the 21st Century" (paper presented at the Proceedings of the 41st Annual Adult Education Research Conference, Vancouver, BC, 2000), accessed January 1, 2013, http://newprairiepress.org/cgi/viewcontent.cgi?article=2250&context=aerc; Ralph G. Brockett et al., "Two Decades of Literature on Self-Directed Learning: A Content Analysis" (February 4, 2000), accessed January 1, 2013, http://eric.ed.gov/?id=ED449348; Stephen Brookfield, "Self-Directed Learning, Political Clarity, and the Critical Practice of Adult Education," *Adult Education Quarterly* 43, no. 4 (December 1, 1993): 227–42; Sharon Bauer Colton, "Developing an Instrument to Analyze the Application of Adult Learning Principles to World Wide Web Distance Education Courses Using the Delphi Technique" (Ed.D. diss., University of Louisville, 2002); Barbara A. Frey and Susan Webreck Alman, "Applying Adult Learning Theory to the Online Classroom," *New Horizons in Adult Education and Human Resource Development* 17, no. 1 (2003); Lucy Madsen Guglielmino, "Development of the Self-Directed Learning Readiness Scale" (Ed.D. diss., University of Georgia, 1977); Merriam, "Andragogy and Self-Directed Learning"; Liyan Song and Janette Hill, "A Conceptual Model for Understanding Self-Directed Learning in Online Environments," *Journal of Interactive Online Learning* 6, no. 1 (Spring 2007): 27–42.

- Use friendly, informal writing style.
- Make weekly announcements or updates.
- Establish weekly online office hours.
- Assure learners that discussion board postings are being read.
- Provide information for telephone, fax, and U.S. post mail.
- Limit class size to allow for effective management.
- Consider using a TA to monitor discussion boards or team discussions.
- Be clear and succinct.
- Prepare students for working in small groups or team by providing objectives, assigning roles.
- Require regular participation for credit.
- Encourage students to respond as well as post.

4. Provide learner flexibility and control:

   - Use asynchronous email and discussion boards for anytime/anyplace participation.
   - Chunk learning into small manageable units or subunits that can be completed in relatively short amounts of time (learners will constantly be coming and going into the course—they need logical stopping/starting points).
   - Allow learner choice of assignments, projects, or research topics (consider learning contract).
   - Incorporate text "signals" such as "this is a long unit," "this is a very important concept," "proceed to Lesson 6."
   - Allow students early access to the course and mail the syllabus several weeks before the course begins.

5. Incorporate motivational strategies to encourage students:

   - Tell why the topic or link is important.
   - Provide practical information with examples.
   - Link new topics to what has already been discussed or read.

6. Offer a variety of forms of learner support:

   - Consider a cohort group that completes program as a group.
   - Provide technical support.
   - Provide learning skills support.

- Provide cohort support.
- Provide departmental support.

7. Maintain the focus of content within units:
   - Provide objectives and an outline at the beginning of each unit.
   - Limit hyperlinks to only a few of the very best.
   - Place additional links at the end of units for enrichment.
   - Summarize key points of units and discussions for closure—debrief, then refocus on the next topic.

8. Provide consistency among courses:
   - Maintain the same format throughout program (i.e., all assignments found under the same course heading).
   - Create PDF printable files of long articles.
   - Use the same headings throughout each unit (perhaps objectives, introduction, content or lecture notes, readings, activities, optional resources, conclusion).

9. Consider the limitations of adult learners:
   - Maintain large, easy-to-read fonts.
   - Use clear, bold colors.
   - Use a variety of graphics, images, tables.
   - Consider different learning styles.
   - Be aware of ADA compliance guidelines.

10. Respect learner roles and life experiences:
    - Assume role of facilitator more than "expert."
    - Recognize diverse backgrounds of adults.
    - Apply concepts to tasks or problems.
    - Use a friendly, first-person style of writing.
    - Ask for introductions that include professional background and some personal information (also provide this type of introduction).[17]

---

17 Frey and Alman, "Applying Adult Learning Theory," 10–11.

What is known of the typical online learner should directly impact best practices for online learning. This knowledge serves as a baseline for an understanding of the identifiable best practices for online learning.

Online Best Practices That Incorporate Adult Learning Theory

What are the identifiable best practices for online learning? Given an understanding of the adult online learner, best practices for online learning should combine the worlds of online instruction with adult learning theory.

A foundational work in the area of good practice for education is that of Chickering and Gamson.[18] Because of their popularity, their seven principles have become a benchmark for online programs as well.[19] The seven principles are that good practice:

> (1) encourages student-faculty contact, (2) encourages cooperation among students, (3) encourages active learning, (4) gives prompt feedback, (5) emphasizes time on task, (6) communicates high expectations, and (7) respects diverse talents and ways of learning.[20]

In 2004, Keeton compared best practices for online courses to that of face-to-face instruction.[21] His article, through extensive research, developed eight principles for adult education. These principles partially overlap Chickering and Gamson's seven practices. One of the most useful outcomes of the research was the development of an instructional practices inventory. He expands on each of the eight principles

---

18   Arthur W. Chickering and Zelda F. Gamson, "Seven Principles for Good Practice in Undergraduate Education," *Biochemical Education* 17, no. 3 (1989): 140–41.
19   Charles Graham et al., "Seven Principles of Effective Teaching: A Practical Lens for Evaluating Online Courses," *Technology Source* (January 2001), accessed January 1, 2013, http://eric.ed.gov/?id=EJ629854; The Institute for Higher Education Policy, "Quality on the Line, Benchmarks for Success in Internet-Based Education," *Tribal College* 13, no. 3 (March 31, 2002): 50.
20   Chickering and Gamson, "Seven Principles for Good Practice," 140–41.
21   Morris Keeton, "Best Online Instructional Practices: Report of Phase I of an Ongoing Study | The Sloan Consortium," *The Journal of Asynchronous Learning Networks* 8, no. 2 (April 2004): 75–100.

for adult education, giving the instructional designer a map for more effective course creation:

> (1) Make learning goals and one or more paths to them clear. (2) Use extensive and deliberate practice. (3) Provide prompt and constructive feedback. (4) Provide an optimal balance of challenge and support that is tailored to the individual student's readiness and potential. (5) Elicit active and critical reflection by learners on their growing experience base. (6) Link inquiries to genuine problems or issues of high interest to the learners (thus enhancing motivation and accelerating their learning). (7) Develop learners' effectiveness as learners early in their education. (8) Create an institutional environment that supports and encourages inquiry.[22]

Bangert used the seven principles of Chickering and Gamson to develop an online teaching evaluation instrument.[23] Student evaluations are not unusual, but Bangert argues that the typical evaluations designed to give instructors feedback do not address these seven principles of good practice. Seven helpful hints are also given in a 2005 article on the research of how to teach online:

> (1) Provide helpful resources on the course site. (2) Let students have control over the pace at which they move through the course. (3) Have lots of discussions. (4) Provide timely feedback to students about their performance. (5) Provide technical support for students. (6) Online study aids and step-by-step presentation may not make much difference in achievement. (7) Evaluation can be enhanced in online courses.[24]

The literature on the best practices for online learning generally falls into two categories. The first category addresses course design.[25]

---

22   Ibid., 96–98.
23   Arthur W. Bangert, "The Seven Principles of Good Practice: A Framework for Evaluating On-Line Teaching," *Internet and Higher Education* 7, no. 3 (January 2004): 217–32.
24   Mary K. Tallent-Runnels et al., "How to Teach Online: What the Research Says," *Distance Learning* 2, no. 1 (2005): 21–27.
25   In addition to works already cited, see also Joan Thormann, *The Complete Step-by-Step Guide to Designing and Teaching Online Courses* (New York:

The second category speaks to quality of instruction. Much of what falls into this category has already been highlighted; however, when the course design is already in place, the role of the professor, as it relates to the established general online best practices, involves mainly providing quality of feedback on assignments, making weekly announcements, responding promptly to email, and facilitating group discussions. The best practices for online learning are those that factor in principles of adult learning theory, instructional design, and quality of instruction. However, another category to review in relation to best practices for online learning is policies and regulations for accreditation.

Online Practices and Accrediting Agencies

How do policies and regulations in the area of accreditation fit into best practices? Several accrediting agencies outline policies and regulatory procedures regarding best practices. In the requirements of affiliation and standards for accreditation, the Middle States Commission on Higher Education makes certain stipulations that go beyond general learning theories, instructional design, or quality of instruction recommendations. The Middle States Commission on Higher Education gives a summary of their expectations with regard to "fundamental elements of distance education, distributed learning, and correspondence education."[26] Lists such as these from established accrediting agencies, with regard to program and course integrity, are worth noting. Distance courses must meet institution-wide standards for quality with regard to instruction, student learning, rigor, and effectiveness. All should be comparable to residential counterparts when applicable. Courses must be consistent with the school's mission. Distance programs must be thought through in all legal aspects. Distance

---

Teachers College Press, 2012); Marjorie Vai, *Essentials of Online Course Design: A Standards-Based Guide* (New York: Routledge, 2011); Nichole Vasser, "Instructional Design Processes and Traditional Colleges," *Online Journal of Distance Learning Administration* 13, no. 4 (December 15, 2010), accessed January 1, 2013, http://www.westga.edu/~distance/ojdla/winter134/vasser134.html.

26 Middle States Commission on Higher Education, *Characteristics of Excellence in Higher Education: Requirements of Affiliation and Standards for Accreditation* (Philadelphia: Middle States Commission on Higher Education, 2011), 58.

programs must clearly identify and communicate appropriate program learning outcomes. Distance courses must be offered often enough to allow students to finish their programs in a stated timeframe. Beyond specifics of courses and programs, the guidelines also stipulate standards with regard to academic integrity, learning resources (such as an online library), faculty training, infrastructural support, and resource analysis.[27]

In a 2012 policy statement by the Southern Association of Colleges and Schools Commission on Colleges (SACSCOC), similar guidelines are given. The need is communicated for schools to be able to verify that students who register are indeed the students taking the courses. A general statement is made that distance education should adhere to *The Principles of Accreditation*, which is essentially their manual for accreditation.[28] However, after this general statement, more specific policies are developed with regard to issues uniquely characteristic of distance education. Similar to the Middle States Commission on Higher Education, they deal with faculty oversight, use of technology, support services, program length, and compatibility with the school's mission. Additionally, accrediting agencies, such as SACSCOC, have asked that the school determine a sound practice for determining equivalence to a residential semester hour.[29]

In the area of theological education, the Association of Theological Schools initially had given specific guidance with regard to distance learning in part five of their *Handbook of Accreditation*.[30] First, as with

---

[27] Ibid., 58–59.

[28] Southern Association of Colleges and Schools Commission on Colleges, "Distance and Correspondence Education: Policy Statement," accessed September 3, 2013, http://www.sacscoc.org/pdf/DistanceCorrespondenceEducation.pdf (), 1–2. This policy statement is intended to supplement "The Principles of Accreditation" by specifically addressing distance learning policies. Idem, "The Principles of Accreditation: Foundations for Quality Enhancement," accessed September 3, 2013, http://www.sacscoc.org/principles.asp. This manual is an extensive guide on accreditation procedures.

[29] Southern Association of Colleges and Schools Commission on Colleges, "Distance and Correspondence Education," 2.

[30] The Association of Theological Schools: The Commission on Accrediting, "Educational Standard," accessed June 13, 2017, https://www.ats.edu/uploads/accrediting/documents/educational-standard.pdf.

the others, all standards that applied to residential courses and programs also needed to apply to distance programs. They should have also stressed the need to verify that students who registered were the same students who did the course work. In addition, ATS required the programs to be compatible with the school's mission and provide for faculty development.[31] However, two other standards were mentioned that stood out as unique. First, ATS was concerned specifically about the standard of theological curriculum.[32] A second unique feature was a statement that prohibited distance courses from constituting "a significant portion of a degree program."[33] Interestingly, ATS seems to be backing away from this policy, and it is beginning to allow for fully online graduate programs. There are even some schools that have been granted an exception that allows them to offer a fully online master of divinity program.[34] Neither of the other accrediting agencies reviewed seemed to indicate any kind of limitation as to whether or not an entire program can exist online.

Conclusion

If education in general tends to consider the needs of the learner, why should online learning be any different? The unique features of online learning have more to do with the online learners themselves than the digital platform. Demographic statistics help the educator understand that online learning is growing steadily and, more importantly, is made up largely of adults that are older than the conventional age for college (eighteen to twenty-four). Given that the average age of the online learner is thirty-four, theories related to how adults learn are highly relevant to any discussion on best practices for online learning.

In addition to considering the nature of adult learning and its impact with regard to online learning, there is the matter of best practices. Literature that deals with best practices for online learning tends

---

31 Ibid., ES.4.
32 Association of Theological Schools, "General Institutional Standards," Standard 3.
33 Ibid.
34 John Dart, "Seminaries Expand Online Options," *The Christian Century*, September 12, 2013, accessed July 30, 2014, http://www.christiancentury.org/article/2013-09/seminaries-expand-online-options.

to build on already-established best practices in education. Institutions of higher learning should consider the importance of quality course design. The course design is usually the first impression for the student. Ease of navigation, clearly spelled-out assignment instructions, a course schedule with due dates, and an organized syllabus are just a few of the standard items in a well-designed online course. Some schools even have dedicated divisions that oversee course design. Just as important is the instructor of the online course. According to the available best practices, an instructor that communicates frequently with students and gives substantive and timely feedback demonstrates just a couple characteristics of an exemplary teacher. Institutions of higher learning should have a careful selection, training, and job performance accountability process in place for the role of the online instructor. Of course, the research available for general best practices does not discuss the biblical and theological qualities of an exemplary teacher discussed in section 2. However, the world of best practices and the world of biblical and theological foundations are not opposites. They can and should be complementary.

Finally, accrediting agencies speak to matters of policy and procedure. These prescriptions guard the integrity of academic programs by ensuring comparability between residential and online programs, by establishing rigor, and by requiring assessment that reviews courses and programs to ensure that outcomes are being met.

So, before discussing best practices for online theological ministry training, schools must decide that they will follow generally accepted best practices that design courses and programs around the online learner. Critical mistakes can jeopardize the most well-intentioned efforts. Professors who may thrive in a live classroom environment due to their mastery of content and engaging personalities are not guaranteed success when it comes to online learning. In the online classroom, weaknesses in the area of pedagogy are far more easily exposed. On the other hand, schools that are committed to excellence in the area of general best practices for online learning are more prepared to succeed at incorporating practices specifically related to theological ministry training.

Opportunities for Application

Discover

1. Analyze current and prospective students in order to learn relevant information that could be useful for course design.
2. Perform some self-assessment in order to discover if one's online courses are in keeping with best practices as they relate to course design.

Decide

1. Determine what measures or systems should be in place to ensure effective course design.
2. Choose the appropriate factors that should influence who is qualified to be an online instructor.

Do

1. Implement an effective training system for online instructors. (This is not necessarily subject-matter training, but learning management system training and policies and procedures training.)
2. Install an accountability system. (Who is going to contact *that* professor when final grades are overdue or when students complain?)

CHAPTER 9

Best Practices for Online Ministry Training

What are the best practices for ministry preparation in online theological education? In order to answer that question, two primary topics must be addressed. The previous chapter discusses the first topic—online learning in general. That topic and chapter have to do with the mode of delivery. This chapter will focus more specifically on online *theological* education and address the unique concerns of theological ministry training in an online context. In order to discover the best practices for ministry preparation in online theological education, a panel of experts qualified to speak on this subject was assembled in order to determine if there was consensus among them on what these best practices ought to be.[1]

---

[1] John Cartwright, "Best Practices for Online Theological Ministry Preparation: A Delphi Method Study" 2014, http://digitalcommons.liberty.edu/fac_dis/153. The next two chapters are based heavily on my doctoral research. The link above will give the reader access to the full research document, including all of the data related to these results. As such, the specifics of that research will be limited to what is necessary for the flow of the text, and readers who wish to explore the research further are encouraged to do so.

Best Practices

This research aimed to discover consensus among a panel of experts as it relates to the best practices for ministry preparation in online theological education. In order to discover these practices, experts in the field of online theological ministry training degree programs were consulted so as to learn where consensus existed among the experts in the field of online theological ministry training.

Since the research specifically sought to establish best practices with regard to ministry training in online seminary or graduate programs, only faculty and administrators with experience overseeing and/or teaching in these programs were considered as part of the population. Additionally, since the research relied on experts of like-faith, a brief survey was given to the participants so that they could affirm the characteristics of evangelical Christianity.

A group of seventeen professional practitioners in the field that fit the above criteria were able to view the issues at hand from a vantage point of knowledge and experience.

Additionally, the best practices in this research were built around an existing set of content categories established by ATS for any school desiring to offer a master of divinity.[2] Rather than invent a set of criteria, it seemed best to employ an already-existing objective set of outcomes. If the experts felt as if there were ways to successfully meet these outcomes in online programs, then it would stand to reason that fully online M.Div. programs ought to be considered as normal practice, rather than as an exception to the rule. Ultimately, the aim was to establish a set of best practices for each of the four program learning outcomes (or categories) associated with the ATS M.Div. program. The hope was that a set of best practices could be established whereby each of these learning outcomes could be accomplished in a fully online M.Div. program.

Initially, these experts were asked a series of open-ended questions that sought to discover each participant's position on how to best accomplish each content category in an online program. After participants responded to the questions, they were given an opportunity to

---

2 These were mentioned earlier in the book, but will be discussed at length here.

view other experts' responses and to revise their own responses, if they so desired. These narratives were then analyzed in order to discover the emerging themes among the responses from which a survey would be developed. This analysis resulted in forty-four statements across the four main content categories.

These forty-four statements were developed into a survey that was distributed to the seventeen participants. The survey called for participants to rate each statement on its level of importance as it related to successfully meeting the learning outcome with which it was associated. Participants were asked to choose between levels of importance: 1—not at all important, 2—somewhat important, 3—very important, 4—extremely important. The results of this survey were analyzed to discover whether or not there was consensus among the experts with regard to each statement. Consensus was defined in this round of the research as any question where at least 70 percent of the participants rated a statement as either 3 (very important) or 4 (extremely important). As with round 1, participants had an opportunity to review all responses as well as make revisions to their own. Questions that did not achieve the mark of consensus, or (after an analysis) were deemed statistically unreliable, were removed, leaving thirty statements in total.

A final round of research was conducted in which participants were asked to review the thirty statements that remained. In this survey, participants were asked to "agree or disagree" as to whether each statement contributes to the successful meeting of the content category with which it was associated. In this round, 70 percent "agree" was used as the mark of consensus among the experts. As anticipated, these thirty statements all met the standard of consensus as defined in this research.

Category One: Religious Heritage

The first of the four content categories involved religious heritage. In this area, six practices were discovered that met the definition of consensus:

1. Require a course, or multiple courses, in which the aim is a comprehensive understanding of history, faith tradition, and denominational expression.

2. Integrate content across a variety of courses within the degree program related to a comprehensive understanding of history, faith tradition, and denominational expression.
3. Align the program with the learning institution's mission, history, faith tradition, and denominational expression.
4. Hire faculty that are in alignment with the learning institution's mission, history, faith tradition, and denominational expression.
5. Utilize the student's church community context as a means of teaching the institution's mission, history, faith tradition, and denominational expression.
6. Offer publicly available resources with regard to the learning institution's mission, history, faith tradition, and denominational expression.

Not surprisingly, given that this content category revolved around understanding, many of these statements involved the cognitive domain (require a course, integrate information, publish information, etc.). Participants in the research regularly referred to a required course as a means of teaching religious heritage.

Other more creative approaches were also suggested by the participants. As one participant wrote,

> Online programs can utilize both static and dynamic online resources to develop a comprehensive and distinctive understanding of the history and beliefs of its faith tradition and denominational expression. At its simplest, this might be a web page with links to different blogs, websites, videos, and other online resources that, together, give a detailed picture of the history and beliefs of the program. A more interactive way would be to create a program-specific wiki that program staff, faculty, students, and alumni can all co-create.

In other words, a full embrace of the best practices of online education will open the door for a whole new world of accessible information. It is this author's opinion that this is less likely to happen with a minimalist approach that simply digitizes a residential course. Another participant addressed meeting this learning outcome by including this kind of information as part of the orientation process. Yet another participant offered several creative suggestions that are well worth considering. Those who offer online theological ministry education might consider

> blogging assignments that encourage students to interact with one another, especially in peer-to-peer connection. Many times the professor is a hindrance to peer-to-peer interaction, and if the professor feels that he or she must dominate discussions because they are the expert, they actually end up being a chokepoint for interaction and learning. A connectivist architecture that decentralizes learning so that more peer-to-peer interaction occurs is very helpful for facilitating honest discussion about beliefs and distinctives. Building a wiki together on a particular subject involving faith and distinctives is a great way for all of them to interact on a topic and crystallize their faith and beliefs through critical thought and reflection while building their wiki entries. Guest speakers in a virtual environment, either live streaming or recorded streaming video or audio, is a great way to build supplemental resources that strengthen the learning process.

One of the great values that could be a product of the above approach is the exposure of students to a broader range of perspectives. Another value, of course, is the staying power of active learning.

Two of the statements that stand out as less anticipated were 4 and 5. Although it seemed normal and rational to hire faculty that align with, or at least are supportive of, the learning institution's religious heritage, do schools intentionally view this as an integral part of meeting this particular program learning outcome? As one participant explained, "The key to any institution is its mission, so if the online program seeks to advance the mission, then it is going to cultivate a greater understanding of the denominational background in the minds of its students." Stated a different way by another participant,

> One of the areas that is often overlooked in the development of an online program, and one in which ATS looks to find alignment, is the cohesion between the institution's mission statement and everything that follows. The goals, objectives, and mission of an institution's online program need to align with the institution's mission statement. Thus, an online program

should have a clearly formulated mission statement that reflects the institutional mission. The courses that follow are likely to reflect the institution's faith and denominational traditions, but those who provide leadership of an online program should provide oversight.

If statements 1 and 2 are going to be accomplished, schools that offer online M.Div. programs ought to be especially aware of the importance of online faculty in terms of their alignment with the institution. Working with adjunct faculty who are located at a distance underscores this point, and section 2 of this book strongly emphasizes this.

A central theme throughout the statements discovered in this research is the importance of the student's in-context community as an integral part of meeting the learning outcomes. In this particular instance, the consensus was that one way to meet the religious heritage learning outcome was to utilize the student's church community. The strength of this is that an institution has an opportunity to teach about its own religious heritage while allowing this understanding to be emphasized and reinforced in the student's church.

In-Context Community

The local community (family, friends, work, worship) in the proximity of the student.

The challenge, naturally, is that religious heritage will vary within the typical student body. One participant described residency experiences of his online program as "semester-long residencies completed in a local church context that aligns with our seminary faith tradition and denominational expression." Another participant explained it this way:

> Online students are often situated in contexts where experts reside. These experts may not be the recognized scholarly experts, but may have a wealth of practical knowledge and perspective. Further, the relationship of online students with these local experts is often much longer, deeper, and more personal than those of campus programs, particularly if campus students and faculty are commuting (and not involved in churches together). For local experts, the faith tradition is not an "academic" matter, but a matter for "our church."

As this chapter will explore, experts consider the student's church community context vital, and the area of religious heritage is no exception. Why unnecessarily isolate a student from his or her church community while he or she is studying in an M.Div. program? Is it not at least a little presumptuous to function as if the only place a student can learn about religious heritage is within the academic course? The online model allows for a both/and approach (seminary and church) that could be the ideal scenario, a concept that chapter 10 will explore.

Category Two: Cultural Context

The second content category for ATS M.Div. programs dealt with the cultural context within which the church lives and carries out its mission. In this area six practices were discovered that met the definition of consensus:

1. Solicit student feedback with regard to ministry strategies that are successful or unsuccessful in an effort to keep informed of changes in the culture.
2. Integrate critical thinking assignments across the curriculum that are designed to interact with culture.
3. Employ student-to-student interaction, such as discussion boards, wikis, and blogs, where skills can be developed for understanding and engaging culture.
4. Utilize various technologies, such as social media, as a legitimate means for understanding and engaging culture.
5. Solicit input on pertinent issues from outside organizations, such as churches or advisory boards, in an effort to keep informed of changes in the culture.
6. Integrate a ministry residency experience such as an internship in order to contextualize and apply learning within culture.

One significant observation regarding the list was that only two of the six (3 and 4) do not expect, either implicitly or explicitly, some form of engagement by the students with their culture. In statement 1, students functioned as a sounding board regarding the effectiveness of ministry strategies learned in a course or program. As one participant stated,

> This (in my opinion) is one of the most promising aspects of distance learning in theological education: individuals who are already serving in local congregations are also learning from practitioners and interacting with their fellow student ministers. They can describe what God is doing in their context in real time and can provide immediate feedback when a suggested practice works—or fails—in their setting.

Imagine an approach in education where faculty are constantly fine-tuning their teaching methods to better fit real-life settings, and where fellow students can provide feedback as to whether an issue in a particular congregation is a trend or a unique situation.

Statement 2 seemed to require some level of cultural engagement in that the assignments are designed to integrate critical thinking as a result of interacting with culture. One participant spoke at length with regard to this idea.

> An online program, if done well, can foster the ready inclusion of material that presents students with the cultural realities or structures of our time. It is easy, for example, to use links to news sites, videos (such as YouTube) or other Internet resources. I believe it was Barth who said that we should do theology with the Bible in one hand and the daily newspaper in the other. If cultural realities are understood through online media, an active online professor can lead students to positive engagement.

This, of course, requires an intentional difference as it relates to active engagement among professor and students versus a passive education in which students simply memorize pre-prepared materials.

Statement 3 may not involve students in their own culture, but inasmuch as online courses are likely to be comprised of students from a variety of cultures, any student-to-student interaction is a form of cultural engagement. Or, as one participant put it,

> What incarnational means to the digital disciple is that it can take the form of both virtual and physical. While the Internet was once used primarily for information gathering, it has now shifted to a more relational component. Real relationships,

incarnational or not, do exist. Online programs that use social, digital, and mobile technologies are ones that will facilitate a conversation with those who are increasingly dominating our culture. We think of spiritual formation as an isolated and private experience that I may share with other Christians but which primarily involves my own personal effort.

The online approach cannot only understand but also incorporate an awareness of this broader sense of cultural engagement. Not only can students learn about the cultural engagement that is possible through something like social media, but can actually participate in it as part of the learning process.

Finally, statement 6 appeared to be the most explicit statement with regard to the understanding of and engagement with culture. Whether it was in the form of an internship of some kind, or the utilization of an existing ministry role for a student, the experts in this study indicate a strong interest in the utilization of the students' existing cultural context for this particular learning outcome. The implication of all of the above statements, of course, is that equipping students in the area of cultural intelligence is critical. The narrative responses in round 1 repeatedly drew attention to the value of the student pursuing ministry training without having to move away from his or her community. This sentiment presented itself repeatedly in the research findings. Lastly, in this learning outcome one especially sees how the best general practices of online learning discussed in the previous chapter cannot be divorced from best practices for online theological ministry training.

Category Three: Personal and Spiritual Formation

The third content category for ATS M.Div. programs dealt with personal and spiritual formation, i.e., the providing of opportunities through which the student may grow in personal faith, emotional maturity, moral integrity, and public witness. Ministerial preparation includes concern with the development of capacities—intellectual and affective, individual and corporate, ecclesial and public—that are requisite to a life of pastoral leadership. In this area, eight practices were discovered that met the definition of consensus:

1. Utilize in-context experiences for the practice of and reflection on ministerial service such as mercy ministry, personal evangelism, or preaching.
2. Include reflective assignments on personal and ministry life such as work, family, study, worship, and rest.
3. Incorporate assignments that utilize case studies or problem-based learning.
4. Offer courses that cover various related topics such as spiritual formation, calling, pastoral theology, or leadership.
5. Emphasize faculty as spiritual models when facilitating and leading discussions, wikis, or video chat.
6. Teach and practice guidelines for in-course discussion such as truthfulness, respect, integrity, and maturity.
7. Incorporate in-context field experiences or internships where students can practice ministerial leadership under the supervision of a mentor who will provide spiritual direction.
8. Encourage and expect areas of relational community and reciprocal learning in online courses such as care, connection, communication, and shared faith.

As in the previous two content categories, the idea of utilizing the students' existing context emerged once again in connection with personal and spiritual formation. As one participant stated, "It is the power of real mentors in real churches that takes personal development to a much deeper level." The issue is designing learning activities that properly engage students in their contexts to maximize what I call "God-given learning community." Statements 1 and 7 directly indicated the use of in-context experiences.

Statements 2 and 3 demonstrate the need for reflective assignments that could contribute to meeting the personal and spiritual formation outcome. One participant offered a scenario in which the course would "require the students to participate in works of mercy. The students are to reflect on the experience and write about the outcome of the activity as well as the impact it had on their own lives."

Two ideas emerged from this particular set of statements on the personal and spiritual formation outcome. The reason these are particularly important is because they make the case for the possibility of personal and spiritual formation in an online setting, something that some argue is not possible. First, participants suggested that faculty could act as spiritual models even in an online program, as this book discussed previously. One participant said that "[f]aculty must model the process of living out their faith through a coaching approach to interacting with students." Second, participants suggested that students could learn from one another within an online course or program. One participant recommended several ways that social networking could facilitate such shared learning between students:

> I use Facebook to engage students in habits of theological reflection through a variety of means, including prayers, posts of encouragement, articles, connecting to one another, sharing personal stories and struggles, and invitations to gather on the campus. I have found it to be a powerful medium through which we can share information (intellectual), support one another with words of encouragement (emotional), offer prayer (spiritual), share pictures of our network (social), and engage in appropriate ways of online networking (moral). Students can be encouraged to engage in a limited-time experience of corporate journaling. They can share their reflective journals with the other students in the course as a way of helping them understand the value of the body of Christ.

Though spiritual formation can occur through relationships with instructors and fellow students, a student's entire body of experience should not be ignored. As one participant wrote,

> Students represent a social ecosystem in which they live, minister, and operate. The online program should recognize that system and imbed those realities into the learning experiences. A student's ecosystem is comprised of much more than the seminary alone, and that spiritual and social development are happening in more than one place and as a result of other dimensions like intellectual and social interaction. The dynamics that are part of the relationship between a student and members of their church, individuals within their family, or persons in the workplace can influence the classroom, whether it is online or in person.

Given this reality, those who design online programs should utilize the whole student experience in order to reflect the principles of adult education as well as theological education.

The eight statements in view for personal and spiritual formation show that formation can occur through the course material, students' contexts, interaction between students, and faculty modeling. In this regard, what appeared to separate the online environment from the residential environment (once again) is the additional opportunity for the online students to remain in their community contexts. This theme will be explored more deeply in the next chapter.

Category Four: Capacity for Ministerial and Public Leadership

The fourth and final content category for ATS M.Div. programs deals with the capacity for ministerial and public leadership, which involves theological reflection on and education for the practice of ministry. These activities should cultivate the capacity for leadership in both ecclesial and public contexts. In this area, ten practices were discovered that met the definition of consensus:

1. Enhance courses on the practice of ministry with current materials from pastoral leaders such as textbooks, blogs, or podcasts.
2. Utilize discussion forums, collaborative blogs, video chat, or other student-to-student and teacher-to-student interaction as a vehicle for theological discussion and reflection.
3. Incorporate assignments on ministry practice such as case studies.
4. Evaluate in-context student teaching or preaching using technology such as uploaded video recordings.
5. Offer biblical theology and exegesis courses as part of the curriculum.
6. Train students in auxiliary areas such as professional skills, sacred use of technology, and legal issues in the ministry.
7. Offer a core of courses on various critical theological topics.
8. Include curriculum that addresses theoretical concepts related to ministry practice.
9. Incorporate in-context ministry practice as a demonstration of ministerial and leadership capacity.

10. Incorporate in-context ministry practice as an extension of theological reflection.

The statements for this learning outcome seemed to be particularly heavy in the area of course content. Statements 1, 3, 5, 6, 7, and 8 all fell along the lines of material that can be taught in an online course similarly to how it might be approached in a residential mode of learning. One participant explained that,

> Theological reflection is one area that online learning can enhance. Reading the great theological minds is a good place to begin. Then, specific and directed questions that require the student to reflect on certain areas and topics will help in this area. Ministry practice can be enhanced by requiring the online student to visit blogs of successful pastors and leaders who are skilled in the practice of real ministry. Discussion Boards are another place where online students can interact with fellow students to reflect on theological ideas and practice of ministry.

No one method is comprehensive, but a multi-layered approach is more successful in appealing to a variety of students and in exposing students to a broad spectrum as it relates to ministry.

Statement 2 articulated a means by which students can interact with one another on the material they are learning in a particular course. One participant mentioned this in reference to a course on teaching.

> I teach a course on teaching methods, and it has an online version. I have them teach the class and provide a video recording of it, which they can upload to a file-sharing website such as Google Drive. Then, other students and myself can watch it, using a rubric to provide feedback, and then schedule a one-on-one Skype session between the student and me to share insights and ideas. Hence, learning the practices of ministry is very possible.

From a technological perspective, more is possible today than ever before, and what is listed above serves as a prime example of how online theological education can move far beyond passive learning that is nothing more than a digitized set of notes. Another participant discussed the value of cohort-based programs as a way of enhancing the interaction between students.

> Cohort-based programs offer the opportunity for students to develop a "safe" learning community in which theological reflection can occur. Group projects, blog or forum discussions, synchronous video chats, can all be used as tools to facilitate the exchange of theological ideas. Faculty or instructors can model reflection and synthesis near the beginning of the cohort experience. Such reflection and synthesis are shifted to the students as the program progresses.

There is also a spiritual value to the interaction between students as it relates to this outcome. As one participant explained,

> Christians who study together at a distance have a common bond of connection that transcends physical time and space. The Holy Spirit is purposely unconstrained by physical proximity and freely operates in and through space to accomplish redemptive transformation. Thus, through our union with Christ and our common indwelling by the Holy Spirit, we are endowed with the capacity to be connected to the Trinity and to one another without being constrained by time and space.

The invisible church is a theologically sound apologetic for the possibility of achieving this learning outcome in an online theological program.

Finally, as mentioned in each of the other three learning outcomes, the idea of in-context practice emerged (see statements 4, 9, and 10). The in-context practice of ministry is critical to the accomplishment of this learning outcome, although it is worth noting here that an internship is required by ATS. However, the next chapter will offer suggestions of how schools can move to enhance and improve the conventional internship mode. One participant explained it this way: "What better context to learn pastoral leadership than a student in a pastoral setting, engaged through an online program with others in a similar setting under the tutelage of a professor? While residential opportunities are fantastic, they are artificial—often separated from real-life and real-church settings, into which graduates are placed with little warning."

Conclusion

Although it is doubtful that any single M.Div. program could incorporate every best practice recommended by the experts, these practices can improve online theological ministry programs. However, institutions that offer an online M.Div. should avoid a potential critical error: merely attempting to duplicate the residential approach in an online learning environment. This approach of simply digitizing all of the residential courses without taking into account the general best practices of online learning is flawed on multiple levels. First, as discussed in the previous chapter, online learners are typically in their mid-thirties and learn in ways that are different than their younger counterparts. Second, online learners are less likely to know each other personally. Intentionally designing courses that create a climate of interaction, not merely between the faculty member and students, but also between fellow students, can be an excellent way to accomplish some of these learning outcomes. This is not accomplished as easily in an online setting, and programs that do not account for the online setting and the online learner may very well miss providing a rich environment for the online learner. Third and most importantly, online theological ministry training allows for the utilization of the learner's own community context. This potential was discussed repeatedly throughout the research and appears to be the most significant of all of the results. This opportunity is the single greatest advantage of online learning over the bricks-and-mortar classroom. The next chapter is dedicated entirely to this single issue.

Opportunities for Application

Discover

1. Analyze current online programs of study and courses to learn what, if any, of the best practices in this chapter are being followed. (If you are not currently in an institution of higher learning that offers an online ministry training degree, study other schools.)
2. Take an inventory of your faculty and determine if they have the makeup that fits with what the experts suggest is fitting for acceptable online instruction in this area. (If you are not currently in an institution of higher learning that offers an online ministry training degree, compile a list of protocols that would guide you for hiring practices.)

Decide

1. Determine a realistic course of action that will involve improving online programs of study and courses. Begin with the items that are most critical for your school.
2. Select your best instructors as defined by those who understand online learning and the best practices suggested by the experts in this chapter.

Do

1. Put a redevelopment schedule together that you will follow. Use deadlines for the various phases of course development. Include regular reviews to ensure that the course design is hitting the mark on the best practices you have decided to include.
2. Commission the instructors that you selected for course redevelopments to train other faculty as well as to continually evaluate the course for further improvement.

CHAPTER 10

The Advantage of Ministry Training in Context

Paul serves as an associate pastor at the non-denominational church that his father planted forty years ago. His father, still the senior pastor, recently spoke to Paul about his desire for him to become senior pastor after his retirement. Paul has long dreamed of becoming senior pastor at the church. As he considers his father's offer, he thinks about the seminary degree that he began a few years back. Paul had begun a master of divinity degree, but pressing needs at his home church led him to make the difficult decision to pause his studies. Now that Paul is considering becoming the senior pastor, he desires to return to his studies and finish, but his enthusiasm quickly fades as he considers the challenges of relocating his family for a few years. The thought of parting from this growing congregation in which he has spent much of his life quickly dashes any hopes of completing his seminary training.

Lisa is a mother of four grown children and has been married to Bill (a local deputy sheriff) for twenty-five years. For fifteen years she has served her church as a children's ministry volunteer. Recently, her church's elders asked her to consider filling the recently vacated role of children's minister. Lisa and Bill are recent empty nesters, and Lisa has been praying about God's vision for how she can best serve in her church. The thought of serving as the children's minister excites her.

The only condition for Lisa being officially offered the position is that she pursue advanced ministry training. Like Paul above, she struggles with the thought of moving away from her community and church in which she and Bill raised their four children. Additionally, Bill's role in local law enforcement makes relocating for seminary training unfeasible.

John has been enlisted in the United States Army for seven years. During this time, he has seen combat duty and lost fellow soldiers to the tragedy of war. He has begun to feel the Spirit leading him to consider a career as an Army chaplain, and he knows that becoming a military chaplain requires a master of divinity degree. He considers a few reputable seminaries; however, he cannot commit to a seminary program while deployed overseas. Even if he was stationed near one of these seminaries, the always-imminent possibility of a duty station change makes the chaplaincy dream feel unattainable.

Thirty years ago, each of these three scenarios would have been final as told above, but today all of them could end quite differently. Paul, Lisa, and John can pursue an online ministry training degree without the logistical challenges of relocating or resigning from current commitments. Additionally, one could argue that this combination of pursuing an online master of divinity while remaining in their communities brings advantages that are lost by relocating to a bricks-and-mortar campus. In other words, a master of divinity degree that does not require relocation is not only possible today, but also may be ideal.

This chapter demonstrates that utilizing the online learner's own church and community context gives online theological ministry training an advantage over the bricks-and-mortar classroom.

Distance: Friend or Foe?

The idea of utilizing the present context and ministries of students as a part of the master of divinity program raises a question of strategy. Should seminaries merely work to make online courses as similar to their residential counterparts as possible, or should they look to accomplish the same objectives while utilizing the student's community? Ogilvie gives an eloquent answer to this question: "Wherein lies the 'distance' in distance education? Is the 'distance' between the student and the institution, or between the student and the community one serves or will serve? Such a question challenges our traditional educational paradigms. It would seem that onsite education creates distance between a student and his or her community, and that the opposite may also apply."[1] In other words, as Figure 1 illustrates, one cannot simply argue that online education involves distance and residential programs do not. All seminary education must overcome some kind of distance—either distance from faculty and fellow students (online education) or distance from one's community (residential education). The online student has the disadvantage of distance from a faculty member and fellow students, while having the tremendous advantage of proximity to his or her community.[2]

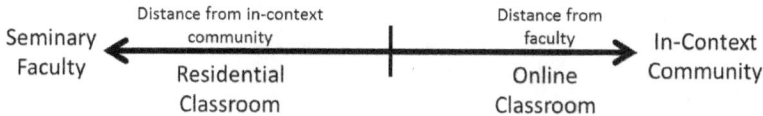

Figure 1: The inevitable distance in all education

In addition to the advantages of convenience, such as not having to move or resign ministries, online students can immediately practice what they are learning in their in-context community. The reasons for choosing online education as the means for receiving ministry training then move beyond pure pragmatism. Increasingly, educators are beginning to recommend intentionally including the student's in-context community as a means of emphasizing and reinforcing learning by way of practice.

Bold as this may sound, online ministry training degree programs can be the option of choice for students. If best practices for online ministry degree programs are fully implemented according to the recommendations by experts in the field, and if full advantage is taken of a student's in-context community, online theological ministry training

1   Matthew Ogilvie, "Teaching Theology Online," *Australian EJournal of Theology* 13 (January 1, 2009), accessed September 18, 2013, http://researchonline.nd.edu.au/theo_article/66.
2   The obvious exception here is when a student is being trained in a residential seminary program that is in his or her local community.

could combine the best of both theory and practice. At the very least, one should acknowledge that the physical distance between a student and his or her professor can be overcome, especially when it is done to minimize the physical distance between a student and his or her in-context community.

Intentional Strategy

Incorporating the student's in-context community does not happen automatically. Rather, incorporating students' community and church contexts as part of the online theological ministry training program requires an intentional strategy. This incorporation is not as simple as requiring an internship (although the internship ought to be included and is greatly beneficial). An intentional strategy must be comprehensive. The following will examine a proposed strategy.

Organizational Structure

Those involved in curriculum development might be tempted to consider modifying course and degree programs as the first option for the inclusion of the student's in-context community (experiential learning). However, what good is a strategy to improve courses and degree programs if the organizational structure and values of an institution are not properly aligned with this initiative? Several components should be considered part of the first course of action.

Mission and purpose. When seeking to include experiential learning in a program, the first consideration should be the mission and purpose of the organization. The mission statement of The Southern Baptist Theological Seminary (SBTS) states in part, "To be totally committed to the Bible as the Word of God, to the Great Commission as our mandate, and to be a servant of the churches of the Southern Baptist Convention by training, educating, and preparing ministers of the gospel for more faithful service."[3] One could easily argue that elements of experiential learning fit very nicely with the mission of SBTS. Therefore, if an institution such as SBTS would seek to offer a

---

3   "ABOUT-from-ST-309-2015-SBTS-Catalog_Web_V13.pdf," 14, accessed December 21, 2015, http://www.sbts.edu/admissions/wp-content/uploads/sites/3/2015/10/ABOUT-from-ST-309-2015-SBTS-Catalog_Web_V13.pdf.

fully online master of divinity program, the leadership would need to be convinced that this mission could be fulfilled by students who are not on location in the bricks-and-mortar classroom. An institution's decision should be rooted in the belief that the mission of the institution can be fulfilled in an online context. The decision should not be a mere pragmatic one in an effort to increase enrollment. Institutions that offer fully online master of divinity degrees cannot treat the online program and its students as second-class when it fulfills the mission statement.

Leadership support. A second component in a successful online program is having engaged leadership. Successful online theological ministry degree programs that make full utilization of the students' in-context community must have the full support of the leadership of the institution. Leaders might give lip-service support to online ministry training programs; however, true approval is proven by their granting authorization and financial support of such programs.

Hiring. A third step in developing a successful online program is the proper selection of both faculty and staff. Institutions must seek out qualified faculty members. Some of this has already been discussed at length in section 2. However, institutions should also select faculty for online master of divinity programs who understand the realities of in-context church experiences. So, beyond possessing the requisite degrees and knowledge in a particular discipline, faculty members must also be able to work with students to facilitate their in-context learning experiences. In addition, an often-overlooked piece of the online learning puzzle is the hiring of staff who can provide the necessary infrastructural support needed for online programs and students. This strategic hiring is necessary for at least three reasons. First, experiential learning staff are able to build strong connections and networks with the various local churches where students in the online program are serving. These relationships are critical, so that the institution can learn how to best support both the students and the churches. Second, experiential learning staff are able to serve as support for students. Third, experiential learning staff can support faculty in online programs. Often adjunct faculty work from a distance and need staff support.

Academic Structure

Once an institution of higher learning has intentionally addressed the organizational needs involved in supporting in-context experiential learning, appropriate attention must be given to the academic aspects of this initiative. There are at least four areas that can be considered. Every institution's approach might be different. However, the hope is that institutions could look at these four areas as recommendations and consider a multi-layered approach that is more comprehensive than any single strategy.

Admissions process. The first recommendation for any institution to consider as part of a comprehensive strategy relates to the admissions process for its students. If a seminary or graduate school is going to include by design a student's own church community as part of the ministry training degree program, then it ought to have some measures to ensure that this student is part of a church community. Granted, many if not most seminaries require some sort of pastoral recommendation as part of their admissions process. However useful a pastoral recommendation can be, it typically only serves as a character reference and perhaps an affirmation that the prospective student is a member of the church. In other words, a pastoral recommendation is great as a way for a seminary to determine if a prospective student demonstrates the kind of character and commitment of one called into the ministry. However, something more is needed if an institution truly desires to take full advantage of a student's in-context church community.

In order to accomplish this goal, an institution must discover if a student's church has a sense of its role in the ministry training process. The seminary and the home church should require more than a simple pastoral recommendation. They should form a partnership. In such a partnership, the church no longer relegates ministry training to seminaries alone, but rather participates in the equipping of ministers. This equipping is done by allowing the student to use the home church as a place where the theoretical lessons learned in the online environment can be practiced. A cooperation between church and seminary in this task will not happen coincidentally. This relationship must be intentional and planned, and therefore it should be a condition for admission into this kind of program.

A seminary with a bricks-and-mortar master of divinity program likely spends much time and energy building a local network of churches and ministries within which students can be involved and gain valuable experience. However, many students will be new to the area and to the churches. A seminary student will arrive as a newcomer to a local church and begin ministering and then move on in three to five years. A major advantage of the online ministry training model is that students can practice in churches with which they have existing and ongoing relationships. This is no small difference.

Learning outcomes. The second recommendation as part of a comprehensive strategy has to do with the desired (and declared) outcomes. Anyone involved in curriculum development in higher learning will recognize these three words: *program learning outcomes*. Some may cringe when they read those words because of painful memories of long hours compiling assessment and comprehensive program reviews. However, accrediting agencies, such as ATS and SACS, require their member schools to state clearly the learning outcomes of a given program. A simple way to understand program learning outcomes is to think of them as what students will know and be able to do as a result of completing a program. This gives any institution of higher learning a means of performing self-assessment. Well-written program learning outcomes can measure success. For member schools of ATS, "These specific learning outcomes should shape and inform the design of all courses, supervised ministry experiences, formation activities, and other instructional strategies to establish a coherent and integrated curriculum for the degree program."[4]

Another way to understand learning outcomes is to see them as a target at which an institution is aiming while designing the various components of the degree program. The success of the program is determined by whether or not students achieve that outcome. Therefore, institutions that offer online theological ministry degree programs ought to find a way to design learning outcomes in such a way that online students succeed.

Developing sound learning outcomes is itself a learning process. Fortunately, many resources exist for inexperienced developers of

---

[4] Association of Theological Schools, "Degree Program Standards," A.1.3.2.

outcomes. Here are some general principles. First, develop outcomes that do not overly depend on one single course in the program. For example, for a learning outcome related to sound exegesis, do not depend on a single course on hermeneutics. Rather, offer a variety of courses where the topic of biblical interpretation might be introduced, emphasized, or reinforced. Likewise, even if a master of divinity program might require an internship or practicum, the internship should serve as one of several means for demonstrating a particular outcome. In other words, suppose a program learning outcome touched on a student's capacity for ministerial leadership. An internship would be an obvious choice for assessing whether or not the outcome is met. However, that outcome could be met in a variety of courses that might require some experiences on site at a local church. One reason for this is that internships are often the culmination of a student's programs. To discover at this point that a student is glaringly weak in an area leaves little time to address the deficiency.

Institutions developing program learning outcomes should also have an intentional strategy for assessment of such outcomes in experiential learning. One approach could be simply asking how each learning outcome could be fulfilled, at least in part, during some facet of in-context experiential learning. This leads to an examination of how to imbed the in-context experiential learning into the courses themselves.

Course integration. As mentioned earlier, most institutions use an internship or supervised ministry experience to provide an experiential learning component for a degree program. While tried and true, this approach has two potential problems.

First, as mentioned earlier, internships tend to be a final, or at least a very late, step in the program. They tend to be treated as a culmination. If this is the student's first required experiential learning step in the degree program, it is almost too late if significant problems or weaknesses are exposed. Internships still have value, but they are more meaningful if experiential learning has been a normal requirement for the student along the way.

Second, the single course approach unnecessarily places experiential learning in a silo within the degree program. How successful would mathematics curriculum be if addition or subtraction were taught once in a class, but the concepts were never revisited again? Or, imagine creating a biblical worldview course as part of a degree program, but then never discussing biblical worldview again in the program. Certain valuable learning experiences are so important they ought to be introduced, emphasized, and reinforced (where possible) all through the curriculum. Experiential learning within the student's in-context church community is an example of a learning experience that should be threaded throughout the online theological ministry degree program.

The following are some ways that in-context learning experiences can be integrated. As a matter of organization, these suggestions will follow the four content categories associated with the ATS master of divinity program standards around which the best practice statements were organized in chapter 8. Additionally, several of those best practice statements will be revisited here.

Category One: Religious Heritage. The first of the content categories involved religious heritage. ATS states that the program should provide students structured opportunities to develop a comprehensive and discriminating understanding of the religious heritage. Among ATS's best practices to attain this outcome, one of those practices directly mentions the student's church community. The ATS recommendation states, schools should "utilize the student's church community context as a means of teaching the Institution's mission, history, faith tradition, and denominational expression."

Students could be required to find and evaluate their church's own faith statement, perform a study on their church's history, or even conduct interviews with some of the ministerial staff. This kind of integration moves the learning out of the silo of the traditional academic environment and into the actual lives of the students as well as the faith communities of which they are a part. The exercise could also benefit the church.

Category Two: Cultural Context. The content category for ATS master of divinity programs deals with cultural context. ATS states that programs should provide opportunities to develop a critical understanding of and creative engagement with the cultural realities and structures within which the church lives and carries out its mission. In this area, several ATS best practices could be realized in local contexts. These include:

1. Soliciting student feedback with regard to ministry strategies that are successful or unsuccessful in an effort to keep informed of changes in the culture,
2. Integrating critical thinking assignments across the curriculum that are designed to interact with culture,
3. Soliciting input on pertinent issues from outside organizations, such as churches or advisory boards, in an effort to keep informed of changes in the culture, and
4. Integrating a ministry residency experience such as an internship in order to contextualize and apply learning within culture.

The first recommendation has potential of providing an insightful barometer to test how well seminaries are engaging their surrounding culture. Students in real-world cultural scenarios can test the theoretical concepts taught in class and provide feedback on what works and does not work in their culture. This requires some humility on the part of the educator, and any kind of know-it-all posture would stifle the benefit of this best practice statement. Statement 3 is similar to statement 1, but instead of testing concepts taught in class, students are soliciting feedback from churches and other ministry organizations in an effort to remain informed about what is happening in culture. Students have the opportunity to learn about other cultures as they hear from other students, and professors have the opportunity to learn from their students. Statement 4 touches on ministry internships. Internships provide a longer, more focused learning experience in which students are given the opportunity to take what they have learned and contextualize it for their ministry settings. The odds of success here are greatly improved because the students are likely to have not left their own cultures to go to seminary.

Category Three: Personal and Spiritual Formation. The third content category for ATS master of divinity programs deals with personal and spiritual formation. Programs should provide opportunities through which the student may grow in personal faith, emotional maturity, moral integrity, and public witness. Ministerial preparation should include the development of capacities—intellectual and affective, individual and corporate, ecclesial and public—that are requisite to a life of pastoral leadership. In this area, the student's church community is essential.

1. Utilizing in-context experiences for the practice of and reflection on ministerial service such as mercy ministry, personal evangelism, or preaching.
2. Incorporating in-context field experiences or internships where students can practice ministerial leadership under the supervision of a mentor who will provide spiritual direction.
3. Encouraging and expecting areas of relational community and reciprocal learning in online courses such as care, connection, communication, and shared faith.

The first recommendation is a classic example of allowing the students to incorporate current ministry practices into the courses of their degree program. The advantages are that students are able to capitalize on what they are already doing, and students are led to connect intentionally their areas of service to their own spiritual formation. The next statement deals with internships, which are directly related to the spiritual growth of students. Internships should not be viewed exclusively as an opportunity to gain ministry experience. Internships should also provide students spiritual guidance under mentors. This mentorship is even more beneficial when the student is already known by the ministerial leadership of a church—a situation far more likely for online students.

Category Four: Capacity for Ministerial and Public Leadership. The fourth and final content category for ATS master of divinity programs deals with the capacity for ministerial and public leadership. ATS states that programs should provide theological reflection on and education for the practice of ministry. These activities should cultivate the capacity for leadership in both ecclesial and public contexts. Those best practices that directly mention the student's church community as a means of achieving this learning outcome are referenced below.

1. Evaluating in-context student teaching or preaching using technology such as uploaded video recordings.

2. Incorporating in-context ministry practice as a demonstration of ministerial and leadership capacity.
3. Incorporating in-context ministry practice as an extension of theological reflection.

Consider the limitations of a homiletics class in a bricks-and-mortar classroom. Imagine how the experience of preaching could be enhanced in a real-life setting. By adding the dynamics of a real congregation, with real parishioners who have real needs and life crises, preaching feels less like an assignment for a grade and more like real ministry. Modern technology allows for those experiences to be recorded and uploaded for the professor to assess, thus bringing both the academic and experiential worlds together in a single experience. Statement 2 above can be fleshed out in a variety of ways. A student could assist in the leadership of a particular initiative or attend and participate in leadership meetings. Statement 3 above is particularly exciting. The student could integrate theological reflections from the online classroom into a real-life ministry setting.

Internships. Also known by other names—such as a residency or practicum—internships are often the final student experience in a degree program. Students spend a semester, sometimes an entire year, in some sort of official capacity within a church or ministry. Every one of the four content categories for ATS master of divinity programs could be fulfilled through such an internship. However, as mentioned earlier, since the internship often comes at the end of a degree program, these learning outcomes ought to be reinforced by these focused experiences. The internship is not the place to introduce concepts but to repeat them by way of practice. In-context ministry practice should be integrated into the program all along the way. In a bricks-and-mortar setting, the challenge is always in finding a partner site that is willing to take on a student intern. This is less of a problem in the online setting in which a student interns in his present ministry.

Conclusion

Online ministry degree programs have the potential to be the option of choice for students. Online theological training can combine the best of both theory and practice, achieving the desired learning outcomes. Although there is distance between the students and faculty members, the close proximity of the students to their own communities could prove to be a great advantage over the bricks-and-mortar setting.

A single advantage has emerged that distinguishes the online seminary degree from the bricks-and-mortar seminary degree: the ability to pursue a master of divinity degree while remaining in the home ministry context. This is no small matter. It allows seminaries to pursue new ways in which ministry degree programs can be delivered.

Seminary, unlike the church, is not an institution ordained by God. Yet, in a very short period of time, the notion has developed that a student must relocate to a residential campus in order to receive adequate ministry training. There was a time when those who desired seminary training had to consider resigning from their jobs and moving their families. With this came the challenge of resettling into brand-new communities and the burden of finding employment. Today, however, advancements in technology allow for learning online in a manner that can be integrated with the student's in-context experience.

Opportunities for Application

Discover

1. Analyze the current admissions process of one's institution in order to learn what kind of partnerships exist, or can exist, with the churches of which online students are members.
2. Take the time to learn whether or not one's institution is set up with the staff support to adequately network with these in-context ministries.

Decide

1. Determine a realistic course of action that will involve integrating into the curriculum in-context ministry experiences that recognize the local church as a context for theological education.
2. Redesign program learning outcomes in degree programs so that contextualized ministry experiences are required by design in every course.

Do

1. Redevelop key courses in which assignments will be included that require students to utilize their in-context ministry setting.
2. Develop an internship that builds on in-context ministry practices that have been included throughout the program.

CONCLUSION

To Teach, to Delight, and to Persuade

The fourth-century theologian Augustine of Hippo once wrote, paraphrasing Cicero, that teachers should express themselves "so as to teach, to delight, and to persuade." He further states, "To teach is a necessity, to delight is a beauty, and to persuade is a triumph."[1] Augustine went on to point out that the first of these—teaching—concerns primarily *what* the teacher does, while the other two relate to *how* the teacher accomplishes this task. Without theological reflection and critique, online theological education can easily be reduced to mere transfer of information. When this happens, seminaries lose sight of the spiritual formation and transformation that can be cultivated in ourselves and in our students when we learn not merely to convey theological data but also foster persuasion and delight. What we have unfolded in this book is a more comprehensive vision for online ministry training—a vision that is theologically grounded, focused on spiritual formation, and integrated with the life of the local church.

This book began with one pressing concern and three questions for practices of online ministry training. Our concern was that in many seminaries and ministry-training institutes, the rush toward

---

1   Augustine of Hippo, *De Doctrina Christiana* 4:12 (27).

online theological education has been driven not by careful theological reflection but by profit-centered pragmatism and adaptation to cultural trends. What the authors of this book have demonstrated is that while some institutions may indeed be making this shift for purely pragmatic reasons, the movement toward online learning is not devoid of theological foundations and considerations. In fact, the perceived presence of apostolic writers through their epistles demonstrates the possibility of significant theological formation through media. Furthermore, more careful consideration of theological anthropology can positively shape practices of faculty development and student spiritual formation in online programs.

Two of the pressing questions that we asked at the beginning concerned the students' context: *How will we teach students to value place if students and faculty are never together in the same place?* and *How will we effectively partner with the student's local church so that this congregation becomes the student's primary context for formation as a minister?* The answers to these two questions are tightly intertwined. The crucial point we have made in *Teaching the World* is that, at its best, online theological education should create a learning community in the student's context. Past attempts to engage online students in the experience of community have typically tried either to connect students virtually to a physical campus or to create a sense of community through online connections. Authentic community, however, requires personal presence. As such, attempts to create virtual connections or virtual community are incomplete, even at their best. The solution we have suggested is the creation of curriculum that carefully and deliberately turns the student's place of ministry into the primary context and community for the application of what he or she is learning.

Practices of online pedagogy should, at their best, train students to understand and to value their places of ministry; this can happen through training that is intentionally adapted and applied in the context of the student's local church. When this happens, online ministry training programs do indeed value place—specifically, the place of the local church. Such an approach gives preference to students being in the same place as their pastors and fellow church members, while simultaneously providing opportunities for them to interact with seminary faculty through online forums or in compressed on-campus experiences. This practice does not aim to minimize the bricks-and-mortar experience at a seminary; instead, it seeks to improve the partnership between the seminary and the local church so that students delight in the role of Christ's church when it comes to ministry training.

One last question concerned the development and deployment of faculty: *How will we select, value, and equip faculty for a task that requires more time and engagement than an on-campus class?* Fair compensation, equitable treatment, and thorough training are excellent places to start. But, for institutions whose mission is to train God-called ministers, there is a higher standard and a higher calling. The institution must also prioritize the online faculty member's theological fidelity and spiritual formation. Standards related only to technological and pedagogical competency are insufficient, because the role of the online faculty member extends far beyond efficiently managing an online classroom. The faculty member must be a model of spiritual formation into the image of Christ, and one responsibility of the seminary is to foster this formation. This must be a central commitment of the institution not only for full-time on-campus faculty members but also for online and adjunct faculty. A faculty member who is being thoroughly equipped and spiritually formed is more likely to become an instructor who delights in the task of teaching and who persuades students to delight in the excellencies of Christ. The result will be more faithful obedience to the Great Commission as we endeavor together to teach the world.

Subject Index

A

Andragogy 141–142
Association of Theological Schools (ATS) 10, 18, 19, 24, 54, 108, 111, 115, 148, 149, 175

B

Bricks-and-mortar 136, 137, 167, 170, 173, 175, 180, 181, 184

C

Communication Medium 38, 91, 92

D

Distance Education xi, 3, 5, 6, 7–10, 17, 40, 41, 60, 92, 96, 100, 108–13, 135, 142, 147, 148, 171

F

Formation ix, xii, 8, 11–14, 23, 42, 45, 47, 50, 54–56, 60–63, 70–73, 75, 80, 81, 83, 84, 86, 87, 102, 103, 105, 107, 112–15, 117, 118, 120, 122, 124–30, 161, 162, 164, 175, 184, 185

H

Humility 111, 115–18, 120, 122–27, 129, 178

I

Image of God 70, 73–83, 86, 89, 90, 106, 115, 124, 128, 129
Imago Dei 73, 75–77, 80
In-Context Community 158, 171–73

M

Middle States Commission on Higher Education 147, 148
Ministerial Effectiveness 108, 118–20, 122, 123

P

Pedagogy 61, 62, 72, 84, 95, 96, 100, 104, 110, 114, 141, 184

R

Role of Online Faculty 73, 84, 97, 100, 103, 128, 185

S

Social Presence v, 17, 18, 20, 28, 31, 32, 37–44, 48–50, 71, 103

Southern Association of Colleges and Schools Commission on Colleges (SACSCOC) 148

Spiritual Formation 10, 61, 72, 107, 108, 110, 112, 113, 117, 161, 178

T

Technology vii, 3, 18, 41, 45, 55, 72, 89, 90, 92–97, 99, 100, 104, 106, 107, 113, 130, 134, 135, 142, 145, 148, 164, 179, 180, 181

Theological Anthropology xi, 72, 73, 81, 84, 85, 89, 99, 108, 184

www.ingramcontent.com/pod-product-compliance
Lightning Source LLC
Chambersburg PA
CBHW021155160426
43194CB00007B/750